Taming the Retirement Octopus:

"Understanding the Fundamentals of Retirement Planning"

Published by
Premier Institute for Financial Freedom

Taming the Retirement Octopus:

"Understanding the Fundamentals of Retirement Planning"

Steven M. Mitchell and Scott Glenn Smith

Cover by: Penny Lane Graphics

Published by Premier Institute for Financial Freedom
1061 Main Street, Suite 19
Banco Park
North Huntingdon, PA 15642

Printed in the United States of America
by
Premier Institute for Financial Freedom

ISBN 1-4243-0703-1

Disclaimer: The material in this book is intended to provide only a broad, general guideline which may be helpful in organizing your financial thinking. As the information provided herewithin is not to be construed as either legal or tax advice, you should consult with an attorney and/or accountant regarding legal and tax implications. No liability is assumed as a result of the use of information contained in this book. It is important to revise your plans periodically in light of any life changes encountered.

Special Thanks...

We would like to give special thanks to the following organizations. Without their help and support this book would never have become a reality.

For assistance in the publishing, editing and design of this book, we would like to thank The Premier Institute for Financial Freedom, and all of the members of their team who helped us turn our ideas into print.

Premier Institute for Financial Freedom
1061 Main Street
Banco Park
North Huntingdon, Pa 15642
www.pifff.org

We would like to thank Financial Profiles for creating and providing all of the financial illustrations used and referenced in this book. We would also like to extend thanks to Financial Profiles for helping to support our planning business throughout the years.

Financial Profiles
5421 Avenida Encina
Carlsbad, Ca 92008
www.profiles.com

For the brilliant design of our book cover, we would like to thank Mr. Bill Dussinger and the company of Penny Lane Graphics.

Penny Lane Graphics, Graphic Design Studio
11 Penny Lane
Lititz, Pa 17543
www.plgraphics.com

To Contact Scott Smith or Steven Mitchell directly, please call or write to:

Planning Strategies, Inc.

A Registered Investment Advisor
900 West Main Street
Mount Joy, PA 17552
1-866-892-5062
www.visitpsionline.com

Table of Contents

About the Authors

In order to understand the premise of this book, you may first want to gain some insight about the authors. Steven M. Mitchell and Scott Glenn Smith are partners in Planning Strategies, Inc., an independently owned financial planning and investment advisory firm located in Mount Joy, Pennsylvania. Along with their partner, Lori Fernandez, they spend their professional lives helping their clients achieve financial peace of mind. While most people only have one retirement experience, Steve and Scott have hands-on experience with literally hundreds of real life retirement stories. It is through these experiences that these authors have learned the empirical lessons that ultimately led to the writing of this book. Unlike the countless scores of "academics" who explain finances from the world of economic theory, Steve and Scott have spent their entire professional careers working with real people, dealing with real problems and challenges, and helping individuals develop the solutions to attain their financial goals. It is this professional life experience that they now hope to bring to you in the pages of this book.

Steven M. Mitchell

Steven M. Mitchell has been actively involved in the finance industry since 1977. After he graduated from Shippensburg University with a business degree, he immediately put his skills to work for the Marine Corps. During his military career, Steve served as an officer and an aircraft/helicopter pilot, flying H-46 assault helicopters and C-12 King Air transport planes. He also spent a year as an air liaison officer with an infantry battalion. In order to further his career, he obtained a Master's degree in finance from Boston University. Upon leaving the Marine Corps, Steve started his own financial planning practice and continued his education. He soon received the Chartered Life Underwriter and Chartered Financial Consultant designations from The American College in Bryn Mawr, PA. Currently, he is continuing his professional development by pursuing an additional Master's degree in financial services from The American College. Steve is the board chairman of the Society of Financial Services Professionals, as well as board chairman of the St. Joseph Health Ministries and serves on the Finance Committee. The primary concentration of his practice is in the areas of retirement planning, qualified/non-qualified retirement plans, portfolio analysis and design, as well as estate and personal financial planning.

Scott Glenn Smith

During the time that Steve was ending his career in the Marine Corps, Scott Glenn Smith was graduating from Penn State University with a Bachelor's degree in Arts & Sciences, with his main focus in the studies of marketing, philosophy and psychology. Scott began his career in the financial services industry immediately after college by attaining his securities and insurance licenses through Prudential Securities. He has been practicing financial and investment planning in this area since 1991. However, Scott will say his career in the investment world actually began long before 1991 because he grew up with a father who spent 35 years as a licensed stock and insurance broker. You could say that investment planning is in his blood. During his career, Scott has continued his professional education in the areas of estate planning, business planning, retirement plans, and portfolio management. He also holds both the Series 7 General Securities License and the Series 65 Uniform Investment Advisor license.

Although their backgrounds and experiences were very different, Steve and Scott quickly learned that they shared the same philosophy of financial planning. Through their working careers within the brokerage and insurance industries, they came to realize that the best interests of the financial institutions were often put far ahead of the needs of the client. They saw that the need to "make the sale" often superseded and reigned sovereign over the best interest of a client. Because of this issue, they developed a very simple rule that would later become the cornerstone principal of their financial planning firm… "Put the plan before the products." Along with their partner Lori Fernandez, they opened Planning Strategies, Inc. exactly one week after September 11, 2001. The fact that this Investment Advisory firm was able to survive, grow, and prosper in volatile times is a testament to their core philosophy that has served their clients well. It is this philosophy that they hope to share with you in the following pages.

INTRODUCTION

This book is an expression of the investment philosophies and strategies that we, Scott Smith and Steven Mitchell, have developed during our years of professional experience. This philosophy is not theoretical in nature. It took form after years of pragmatic analysis and personal involvement in thousands of real life financial journeys. In our years of financial planning experience, we have seen many retirement plans that have provided peace of mind and security. Unfortunately, we have also witnessed the results of many poorly conceived plans that have caused terrible consequences. It is our sincere hope that you will now benefit from the wisdom acquired through our collective experiences.

In the following chapters, we will help you gain a thorough understanding of the fundamental principals of financial planning. You will then be able to apply that knowledge to your own financial planning process. Directing does not mean you do it alone, it means that you control the process, assemble the right team, and pilot the ship. Maintaining control over your own financial destiny and planning for all aspects of retirement are the keys to enjoying a successful future. Ultimately, this is what this book will guide you to do.

You should also realize that this book does not contain any "magic bullets," "industry secrets," or "breakthrough systems to get rich." Many of these wonder books and programs that are on the market do not deliver what they promise. You will achieve a successful retirement as a result of careful planning and initiative. We will be completely honest. Financial planning requires you to make a commitment to your future. If you are willing to accept this responsibility, this book can serve as your guide and instruction manual.

Furthermore, since every individual has unique financial needs and goals, it is important to understand that it is impossible to write a book that contains the perfect financial plan. We admit that we may not even be able to answer all of your questions. As you may know, there are many books and products being sold that claim they offer the perfect solution to your financial planning needs. One of the best ways to know when NOT to follow the direction of an "expert" is when an author or financial celebrity starts to give blanket advice, saying "you should" or "you should never." Who are they talking to? When the self-professed experts are giving advice heard by thousands of people, what do you think the odds are of that advice being correct for even half of them? Should the financial guidance for a 22-year-old college graduate be the same as that of a 70-year-old widow? Certainly not. Everyone needs a customized plan to meet their individual circumstances. One person's solution may not be appropriate for someone else. Because of these reasons, it is very important to learn that there are no absolute do's or don'ts in the financial world. The process of creating financial solutions involves understanding, planning, initiative, and the flexibility to change as circumstances change. In other words, there are no two plans that will look the same.

As we mentioned earlier, this book does not contain any

"magic bullet" secrets to solve all your problems. However, it will clearly outline the steps you need to take and the areas in which you need to focus. This book addresses the fundamentals of creating a financial plan, implementing your goals, and maintaining control over your own financial future. So with that said, let us "meet the octopus!" The title of the book comes from the philosophy that there are eight fundamental arms to a good retirement plan. These eight fundamental areas of planning are as follows:

- Choosing the Right Pension Option
- Social Security/Medicare/Medicaid
- Retirement and Income Taxes
- Maintaining Lifestyle and Not Outliving Your Income
- Managing Risk
- Protecting Your Family
- Preventing Medical and Long Term Care Costs from Consuming Your Retirement Assets
- Basic Estate Planning

These eight planning topics make up the fundamental foundation of a sound retirement plan. For the purpose of being congruent with our title, they will be considered the eight "Tentacles of the Octopus."

In addition to these technical or "planning specific" topics, planning a successful retirement also involves preparing for a major lifestyle change. Many people retire after 30 or more years of living life a certain way. Many individuals define their self-perception and identity to their profession. For some retirees, the abrupt changes that occur can be surprisingly stressful, causing feelings of loss, anxiety, and even depression. Because we have worked with so many individuals that have experienced this reaction, we know the importance of developing strategies to make the transition smooth and stress-free. Although this topic may sound more psychological than financial, a special chapter has been dedicated to this subject so you can see how it relates to your financial future.

It is imperative to understand that just as a chain is only as strong as its weakest link; a financial plan is only as strong as its biggest vulnerability. In other words, a plan that does not address all of the fundamentals is a weak plan. One of the amazing and unfortunate things that we have seen in our years of working in the financial services industry is how consumers will spend so much time and energy focusing on one or two areas of retirement planning, but will completely ignore others. To make matters worse, the areas that are being given the attention are not even on our list of eight. Spending hours finding the least expensive no-load mutual fund or locating the online trading account with the lowest fees will not do very much for you in the long run. Oddly enough, this is where some people spend all of their energy. Consumers are not the only culprits to blame for this oversight. Many "advisors" are just as guilty of this type of myopic focus because they only want to feature the product they are selling or deal with topics in their comfort zone. Some advisors do not network with other professionals who can fill in the gaps when needed. As you read this book, we want you to keep in mind that a sound retirement plan must address all eight fundamental areas and that your team of advisors must be able to provide guidance on all of these topics. If both of these actions do not occur, you are setting yourself up for disaster.

In addition to ensuring that all eight areas receive proper attention, you also need to make certain that they work together and support one another. At times, this can be tricky. This is why you should find an experienced and knowledgeable advisory team who can create a comprehensive and congruent financial plan with all eight areas synergizing with one another. This is how the top professionals earn their fees.

We are going to explore each of the eight "Tentacles" one by one and then we will close this book by discussing how to integrate each discipline into a self-supporting retirement plan. Please understand that each of these areas could have an entire book dedicated to it. The scope of this work is to provide an understanding of the fundamentals, as well as a practical guide for beginning your financial planning journey.

It will become evident throughout the course of your study that properly addressing all the areas of financial concern in a functional and effective way does involve a great amount of care and skill. If it starts to seem overwhelming…take heart. Knowing your desired outcome is half the battle. The information provided in each of the following chapters will show you how to get on and stay on the right track. Once you grasp the basics, you can clearly define the goals and aspirations of your financial plan and know how to get the help you need in each area.

Before We Begin...

As we were organizing the vast array of topics and information that we wanted to present in this book, we thought it was logical to first introduce the subject of how to seek advice and guidance on retirement planning. We will specifically discuss what sources of advice you should use and how you should choose the individual or team that you will rely on for professional assistance.

Perhaps the best way to begin this chapter is posing the question: why should you use a financial advisor?

The amount of services and information available to "do it yourself" investors is staggering and is growing every day. One of the fastest growing areas of the financial services industry is the online brokerage business. These internet sites offer research information, financial calculators, and greatly reduced expense structures for online trading. These services allow you, the investor, to eliminate the middle man and plan your financial future on your own. With these resources available, you may wonder if you really need the help of a professional.

Well, in order to answer that question, begin by considering a few points. Handling your own financial portfolio, making your own financial decisions, and being in control of your own financial plan are all great ideas. In fact, it is our opinion that you should never completely turn over the reins of your financial future and you should never give total control or discretion of your accounts to anyone. However, we strongly recommend that you seek the help and advice of licensed professionals to make financial decisions and to create a financial plan. We believe that the true value of a financial professional is not to put that person in a control position, but rather to utilize them as a valuable resource for information and expertise. We endorse controlling your own financial destiny. However, attempting to accomplish your financial goals without a team of qualified advisors to provide direction and support is not a wise decision.

The best way that we can exemplify this point is by referring to the philosophy of Andrew Carnegie -- a philosophy that has been shared by some of the most successful people in history. This historical figure was one of the most successful and influential giants of industry in this country's history. Carnegie achieved that status by mastering the production of steel and building an empire and fortune in the steel industry. Ironically, Carnegie did not know very much about the actual production of steel. He also did not know anything about managing a multi-million dollar production industry. However, this man did possess a far greater ability. During an interview conducted by a young Napoleon Hill, Carnegie was asked to what one aspect he attributed his success. Without hesitation, Carnegie answered that his great accomplishments were a result of his "master mind alliance." Carnegie did not know how to produce steel, run factories, or mines. Yet, he could manage people who did possess these skills. Carnegie did not spend years learning everything there was to know about the many steps involved in the production of steel. Instead, he hired and surrounded himself with experts who did. As any successful leader would, he spent his time and energy coordinating their talents and efforts. His team consisted of 20 men, and he referred to them as the mastermind alliance. This group of individuals led by Carnegie created the steel industry in America. If you study the lives and careers of influential and successful figures, you will find this same philosophy surfacing again.

At this time, you may wonder how the history of Andrew Carnegie relates to the topic of investing. Well, creating an effective and comprehensive retirement plan requires knowledge of law, tax codes, investments, and finance. A retirement plan also needs frequent monitoring, updating, and maintenance. If you did nothing else for 40 hours a week, you still could not perform all of these tasks as effectively as a team of professionals. The fact that attorneys, tax, and investment professionals all have different educational, licensing, compliance, and regulatory requirements should make it very obvious that one professional will probably not be able to handle all of these responsibilities. If one professional can not handle it all, then neither can you. We suggest that you follow the footsteps of Carnegie by hiring a "mastermind alliance." This does not mean that you should relinquish control of your financial future. In fact, one of the major beliefs that we have instilled in our financial planning practice is that the client is the captain of the team. Our firm provides investment advice because we are licensed professionals. We work in concert with our clients' legal and tax advisors, as well as mortgage specialists, trust officers, lenders, banking professionals, and any other needed specialists. We pride ourselves on building an interdisciplinary team in which all members work towards the financial well-being of the client. Although the team may have several members, there is always only one captain, and that is the client.

We strongly suggest you view the process of retirement planning the same way. You should always be the one making the decisions. However, use the talents and expertise of professionals to assist you in making educated decisions.

Preparing for Lifestyle Change

The majority of this book is all about the financial matters that most people are concerned about at retirement. This chapter, however, is all about grappling with all the seemingly disparate non-financial decisions that we all must make when contemplating our golden years in retirement. In 15 years of working with pre-retirees, as well as retirees themselves, we've come to understand the intricacies and delicate weave of those issues. Although each person's situation is unique, and accordingly requires individual attention and planning, every person faces the issues and decisions we address in this chapter.

In many respects, we have found the topic of this chapter to be the single most important aspect of achieving a successful retirement. Success is usually not measured by dollars and cents, or who has the most and biggest toys, but rather by who is the happiest. The path to individual happiness is usually derived via very different things. Happiness is usually a consequence of those things which we value, and many times they are intangible. Physical assets such as boats, planes, cars, houses, etc. are often just the means to the end value for which we strive. True happiness is usually measured by things like, serenity, family harmony, security, making a difference in your community, etc. Those are all intensely personal, and require a deeper, personal introspection to more fully appreciate and understand the ramifications to your retirement plans. That's not to say there aren't common issues that we routinely address with clients. In reality, many people value many of the same types of qualities. So we'd like to address some of the most important non-financial decisions we all face when looking forward to the day when we can cast off the yoke of employment.

We all dream of the day when we can spend our golden years playing golf on a plush Caribbean island, or whiling away the hours with friends and family, but far too many people ever prepare themselves for the day when they really do retire.

When we ask people what retirement means to them, unfortunately, the answer is all too often a shrug of the shoulders, coupled with some target age. It's funny how the answer we hear today is quite different from what it was prior to the 2000-2003 stock market correction. Perhaps it is because the concept of how to plan for a radical lifestyle change is beyond most people's comprehension, but the bottom line is that we think people are just overwhelmed by the octopus, so it's just plain easier to ignore the monster and deal with it another day. Fred Astaire once said, "Old age is like everything else. To make a success of it, you've got to start young."

In our opinion the key questions to address are the following:

- **Are you prepared financially?**
- **Do you love your job?**
- **How will you fill your time?**
- **Is your spouse ready?**
- **Where will you live?**

Most every book we've seen or read deals with the first question alone. And fear not, as we also plan to pontificate on the question of financial preparedness in great detail as well. But since it is but only one of the five key questions, we felt it only fair that we spend at least the balance of this chapter addressing the other factors of a happy and contented life in retirement.

Do you love your job?

At first glance, this seems like a straight forward and simple question. People used to go to work for a company out of high school or college, and they would stay with that company for forty years until they got the golden watch. Did they love their job, or was their job merely a means to an end? I guess it really doesn't matter anymore because it's rare to find an individual anymore with that type of career pattern. People today change jobs on an average of 7-8 times during their working careers. Workers are on a continuous quest for meaningful, satisfying employment. Assuming that most people eventually find what they're looking for, and I know that's a bit of a stretch, then the answer to the question should be even truer today than in the past.

The question then is, if we love our jobs, why would we ever want to quit working? There are a host of factors, both social and emotional, which we believe drive us to retirement. Age discrimination is still certainly a factor in people finding new meaningful employment as they age. Until our society realizes that some people actually enjoy working past the magical age of 65, employers will continue to discriminate in favor of younger candidates with "longer potential." Health is clearly another consideration. At some point, many people become emotionally and physically "worn out." Although they may want to continue working, the daily stress and grind of employment becomes detrimental to their well-being.

Certainly, the tug of the dream retirement is a powerful influence on our decisions as well. The grass is always greener on the other side. The problem is far too many people are financially incapable of living the dream we set up in our minds. When faced with this dilemma, many people would rather save face than face reality, so they compromise and pretend they are doing what they want. The point is not that we shouldn't dream. Dreams are an important emotional pastime. They provide relief from the stress and burdens of our hectic lives. All too often, in regards to retirement planning however, these dreams are idyllic and unreal. Some people may dream of having the wealth of Bill Gates, but it's not a very realistic goal. Dreaming and goal setting are similar, yet totally different. Good goal setting starts with a dream, but is refined with reality. Now, we know the positive mental reality people are all in revolt at this point, because it appears we're advocating that people should discard their dreams and accept something less than what they want. The real question is what do we really want? Do we really want the wealth of Bill Gates, or is it the freedom and peace of mind that comes with such wealth?

In his book, *Smart Women Finish Rich*, author David Bach suggests an exercise in which you explore the meaning behind what is important to you about money. Through a series of inflections on what is important about your life's values, he proposed that you ultimately get to the root feeling and causes of your financial concerns. We think this technique could also be applied to our dreams for retirement, to help us come up with our realistic goals.

We know some of you are wondering how I went from "do I love my job?" to dreams and goals. The point of this is that, working and retirement are not mutually exclusive, as long as work and your goals themselves are not in conflict. Perception is reality. If you perceive the requirement to work, then it is in conflict with a successful retirement. If however, you perceive work as a fulfilling means of achieving social interaction and enabling comfort, then, it is an important aspect of a successful retirement goal. We love our work and can't even envision a point in time where we won't enjoy helping people win the war for generational financial independence. The point is not whether working is a good or bad thing in retirement, but rather, does it fit in with your overall goals.

How will you fill your time?

The question of how will you fill your time is an extremely important question, both mentally as well as physically. It seems that everyone knows of someone who "retired" and six months later was dead. All too often, boredom and lack of purpose is the real culprit. We feel that the ultimate measure of a successful retirement is how you answer this question. You can't spend 18 hours a day, seven days a week playing golf. There's ultimately got to be some mental and physical stimulation involved with our lives to stave off atrophy. Although the measure of pleasure varies widely from person to person, it ultimately relates to the accomplishment of some goal or an activity which accomplishes a goal. For many people, the retirement dream is usually thought of as some form of entertainment, and rarely thought through to its ultimate conclusion. Entertainment alone rarely consumes one's time to the extent that it is meaningful.

Many of us will be faced with retirements which will last for a longer time than we've spent in our working careers. It is best to begin developing hobbies or pastimes which will be a meaningful endeavor to us. If you assume that you will develop an interest once you retire, then most likely you are doomed to boredom.

Let's go back to Fred Astaire. Even if you've managed to set yourself up financially to: a) have to work and b) you don't want to work, in order to be successful, you must be happy with what you are doing. Just as nature abhors a vacuum, the mind abhors boredom. If work consumes the majority of our time during our working careers we had best plan to replace those hours with a meaningful experience, or the "shock and awe" of massive boredom will surely cause the ultimate atrophy of rigor mortis. What it is that fills those hours is extremely personal and can only be measured by the extent to which it relates to the fulfillment of your personal goals.

Is your spouse ready for you to retire?

A phenomenon which is increasing in frequency is the

divorcing of retirees. When two people, both of which have spent most of their lives out of the house working, suddenly find themselves spending all their time together, the problem of filling their time becomes geometrically harder. There must be a balance struck between the individual and the couple. We do not claim to be marriage counselors or psychologists, but we do suggest discussing this issue with your spouse well before retirement occurs. It may be difficult to imagine at this time, especially if both spouses are working many hours. However, discuss how each of you will spend your time, as well as other interests that you would like to pursue, either individually or as a couple. This is another good reason to develop an interest or hobby. Exploring other interests will allow you to have time to yourself and to maintain a healthy relationship with your spouse. The most successful couples generally find a combination of individual as well as joint activities to fill their time.

Where will you live?

The choice of where you are going to live is another question which is very important and must be given due consideration. Too often the dream is the primary motivator to action, but the consequences are rarely thought through.

Many times the true desires of spouses can be in conflict, and it amazes us always at the extent to which there exists a lack of true communication around this issue between spouses. The dream is often a personal versus a joint dream, especially with respect to where you want it to occur.

Several factors should be given serious thought. Probably the most important factor, which many people underrate, is the proximity to family and friends. We've seen far too many cases where retirees move away to the dream location, only to move back to family within a few short years. Families can provide a measure of security as well as physical and emotional support. They also provide numerous opportunities for activities to help fill the hours.

Weather is often a consideration that is given too strong an emphasis. As we age, those of us in colder climates often grow to hate the winter; with its short days, ice and snow. The Dream usually involves some place where at least we can get away from the bad weather. It's funny though, how many people that do move away to the southern states, often talk of how they miss the change of seasons, especially the spring and fall. Although I'm not sure that's often enough to cause them to change back to living in the North, it certainly points to the over-rating often given to weather in the decision process. Even more telling is the "snow-bird" phenomenon, where more and more people choose to maintain two residences, one in the North and one in the South, and splitting the time spent at each location to take advantage of the best weather in each location.

The last two factors which we believe are all too often overlooked, but can be very influential on the success of retirement plans, are the demographics and economics of a region. These factors include such concerns as cost of living, transportation, medical facilities, entertainment venues, and support structures. Obviously the extent to which these systems are available within a community vary immensely. It seems to us though, whether by accident or happenstance, many communities in this country are moving toward becoming retirement communities. We're not just talking about planned communities of retirement homes, but rather of entire towns and cities that truly cater to the retiree. The perfect examples might be St. Petersburg, Florida or Sun City, Arizona. As the baby boomer generation moves into the retirement years, this phenomenon will grow in size and scope. We may even see entire planned cities in the future.

It is our opinion that all the factors we've spoken about in this chapter are in most respects far more important than the financial issues which represent the balance of this book. The issues presented here are highly personal in nature, and consequently there are no right and wrong answers. We have found though, that it is the extent to which you plan for these factors, and communicate with your spouse about what retirement is going to mean to you, that will often mean the difference between a happy and peaceful retirement and a boring nightmare. Fred Astaire was indeed a very wise and insightful man.

Meet the Octopus
The Eight Tentacles
Last Wil
and
Testamen

Tentacle 1

Choosing *the* Right Pension Option

Tentacle 1
Choosing the Right Pension Option

As time marches onward, fewer and fewer people have a guaranteed pension. As we write this text, there are major problems brewing at several major airlines, most of which relate to the unfunded pension liabilities of the companies, and their inability to meet them. Fewer and fewer companies are willing, or able to accept the responsibility and risks associated with guaranteeing income for the entire life of their retirees. Let's face it, retirement used to mean a whole different thing 30 years ago. Today, it is not uncommon to see people actually living longer in retirement than they spent working! Not many companies can predict their financial viability 30 or more years into the future. It's hard enough to forecast one year out, let alone thirty.

Faced with this problem, the retirement plan most companies now offer is the 401K plan. From a company's perspective, it is a great plan because "what you see is what you get." The company has no future retirement funding requirements, and no liability.

For those of you fortunate to work somewhere that has a guaranteed pension, there looms a giant decision in your future. You see, there are at least three, and quite possibly many more options as to how you can receive that pension once you've retired. The option you choose, which controls the payout you receive, will probably be the single most important financial decision of your entire life. Astonishingly, most people stumble blindly into the decision. To make matters worse, companies will not help their employees or provide any guidance in making that decision because of liability concerns. As a result, this decision is all too often based on the decision that friends and acquaintances that retired ahead of them made. Their own personal situation is not even a serious consideration!

Federal law requires that you must be given options as to how your benefits will be paid. This was enacted to ensure that the spouse of a retiring worker is given due consideration. Numerous variations exist among companies. We will cover the major concepts and explain the benefits and risks associated with each approach.

Because of the proliferation of 401K plans, most people assume that a lump sum payout is going to be an option upon reaching retirement. In reality, because of the nature of a defined benefit plan, a lump-sum payout is seldom offered. This type of plan does not really accumulate an individual account balance for each employee, but rather establishes a "future liability" to pay a stream of income. This means the company must begin saving money to pay for that future liability. In essence, these types of plans operate on the same principles as an insurance company. By diversifying the risk of making payments over a large number of retirees, the actual experience of the plan's liabilities will approximate the standard life expectancy tables.

Just as insurance companies assume some people will live shorter lives than the norm, and some will live longer, so do these types of retirement plans. If the plan allowed lump-sum payouts, the risk to the plan is that all the unhealthy people with shorter life expectancies would choose the lump-sum option, and the healthy people with long life expectancies would elect lifetime payouts. This would clearly place financial stress upon the plan. It could result in failure of the plan, or require the company to make additional contributions to the plan. This scenario is called "adverse selection" in the insurance world, and is of major concern for many companies.

Since you are most likely not able to take a lump sum at retirement, what are you to do? Because this decision process can become very complicated, we recommend that you either do a lot of research, or seek out professional help. This is especially important because the choice you make is generally irrevocable. Being irrevocable means that once you sign on the dotted line, there's no going back and asking to change it. Your unique personal situation is very important in determining the best option for you. Don't make this decision without fully understanding all the ramifications.

There are generally three major pension options:

- Life Only
- Joint and Survivor Life
- Joint and some percentage (Joint and 66%, 50%, etc)

There are variations to all of these options. If you understand how these options work, you will be well prepared to understand how any of the variations will function. Here is a brief overview of each option.

Life Only

This option is probably the least popular option. With it, the retirement plan will make periodic payments (usually monthly) to the retiree for the duration of his/her life. When the retiree dies, the payments stop. This is why many people feel this is an unattractive choice. It does not provide any security for a surviving spouse. The spouse does not receive anything after the retiree dies. However, if the spouse dies before the retiree, the payments are not affected at all. The only thing that matters to the plan, is whether the retiree is alive.

The dilemma here though, is that this option usually will provide the largest monthly income to the retiree. The risk to the retirement plan is defined as the life expectancy of the retiree. The company will probably have to make monthly payments to this retiree until his/her life expectancy – period. All the other payout options involve not just the life expectancy of the retiree, but also the life expectancy of the spouse as well. If two people are involved, the retirement plan will probably be paying the monthly benefit for a longer period of time. Consequently, the plan will have to reduce the amount that is paid out on a monthly basis – so that the expected total payout remains the same. We will walk you through a hypothetical example shortly. But first, let's look at the other two major options.

Joint and Survivor Life

One of the most popular choices is the Joint and Survivor Life option. This option is required by law, and was instituted to protect a surviving spouse. This option pays a benefit for as long as either spouse lives. Unlike the Life Only option, if the retiring spouse passes away first, the surviving spouse continues to receive a monthly benefit. This option ensures that both spouses are protected for the rest of their lives.

The Joint and Survivor option generally offers a smaller monthly benefit. As stated earlier, the retirement plan has to assume they will be making payments to the couple for a much longer period of time. With this option, careful analysis of payout options becomes very important, because companies assumptions regarding spouses can be very disparate. Some companies will look at the actual age of the spouse and calculate actuarially the joint life expectancy of the couple. This determination could either benefit or be detrimental to the retiree. Other companies look at factors such as the age, sex, and degree of age separation between spouses. Other plans might assume the spouse is the same age as the retiree, and may not calculate life expectancies based upon sex. We've even seen companies that subsidize the Survivor option, so that there is not any benefit reduction. Generally though, this option results in the smallest monthly income. Nevertheless, it does afford the best protection for a spouse.

Life and Percentage

This option can best be defined as a mixture of the previous two options. The Life and Percentage option pays a set monthly income to the retiree, as long as he/she is alive. If the spouse dies before the retiree, the payout to the retiree does not change. However, if the retiree predeceases their spouse, then the surviving spouse receives a percentage of what the retiree was receiving. The percentage in the Life and Percentage Option can vary. Many times there are several percentage options presented to the retiree. The most common figures are 66%, 50% and 33%, but this is by no means the only percentages you might see.

The monthly payout amount with the Life and Percentage option usually falls somewhere between the other two options previously discussed. Generally, the spouse will receive an income that is less than the Joint Life payout, because it is only a percentage of the retiree's already reduced monthly income. Although there are certainly circumstances in which this option makes sense, we have seen way too many times where the Joint and Percentage option serves only as a peacemaker. In most cases, the couple really wants the higher income of the Life Only option, along with financial security for the spouse, so they settle on this option. However, this may not always be the best decision for most couples. This option is most appropriate when there are already additional assets available that are sufficient to fund retirement income goals, or when the spouse has his or her own pension benefit.

The following table represents a typical representation of how the options might be presented to a retiree.

Life Only	$2,500 per month
Joint and Survivor	$1,500 per month
Joint and 50% Survivor	$2,000 / $1,000 per month

Joint and 33% Survivor $2,100 / $700 per month

Of course, these three options may not be the only ones offered. Other choices may include "period certain" guarantees, and "partial lump-sum" payments. Each plan is unique, and each has its' benefits and downsides. What is right for one individual could be totally wrong for the next person. Therefore, do not base your decision on what your friends and acquaintances may have chosen. Sadly though, that is what we see as the most common decision tool. In order to make a wise decision, evaluate all your options and seek the assistance of a professional.

As you begin your search for the best pension option, you may have a preconceived notion that you can rely upon your employer for advice. However, most companies will not offer any guidance to their employees, for fear of liability. In addition, our human resources staff is usually not qualified to give financial planning advice. Hence, the potential liability to the company for making a bad decision is enormous, and businesses do want that responsibility.

Remember, if you are married, your spouse is required to sign documents regardless of which option you may choose. This signature indicates that your spouse understands that you have elected to receive the benefit, and that he/she consents to that form of payout. It is very important for your spouse to be included in the planning process, especially since the payout will affect both of you for the rest of your lives.

A related topic we would like to explore is commonly known in the financial services industry as pension maximization. As we discussed earlier, the basis for determining actual payout amounts is essentially an actuarial calculation based on life expectancy and future earnings rates of the retirement plan. Any option other than Life Only, can be viewed as a decision to insure an income for a surviving spouse. Pension maximization introduces the question as to whether commercial life insurance is a more viable solution for guaranteeing an income for a surviving spouse, rather than the retirement plan's options.

The idea is to buy a personal life insurance policy on the retiring employee, and opt for the Life Only payout option. If the retiree dies before the surviving spouse, he or she can receive a life insurance lump-sum benefit, which will replace the income that terminates at the retirees death. Ideally, the additional monthly income provided by electing the Life Only option, should be sufficient to purchase a large enough death benefit. In the example earlier, the $1,000 per month difference between the Life Only payment and the Joint and Survivor option, should be sufficient to buy a life insurance policy on the retiree – that at some assumed rate of return would provide $1,500 per month income to the surviving spouse for the rest of his/her life.

As we mentioned previously, the pension plan options are irrevocable. Once the decision to choose a Joint and Survivor payout is made, you can not change your mind at a later date. Here is an example of why that is so important. Let's say that the spouse dies before the retiree. Using the sample chart above, if the Joint and Survivor option had been chosen, the retiree would then continue to receive just the $1,500 per month for the duration of his or her life. However, in the pension maximization scenario, the retiree would have had more flexibility with a commercial life insurance policy. Not needing the life insurance anymore, the retiree can simply stop paying the $1000 per month premium and can now have $2500 per month to live on for the rest of his or her life.

Here is another aspect of pension plans to which most people don't give due consideration. By definition, all the basic pension options provide benefits to only the retiree and his/her spouse. Children do not receive anything. However, this is not necessarily the case with pension maximization. As stated earlier, the lump-sum life insurance amount should be sufficient enough that when invested properly will provide an adequate monthly investment income for the life of the surviving spouse. The principal lump-sum should never be required to be depleted, or the guarantee becomes questionable. Therefore, there should be a sizable lump-sum amount which is still available when the surviving spouse dies. This amount can then be left to the couple's children, or whomever they desire. For this reason, pension maximization may seem very attractive.

Those are compelling reasons to consider the pension maximization idea, but are by no means the only ideas promoted. There can be many personal reasons for which variations of the basic idea can work, such as using the joint and percentage options, reduced insurance/income needs due to other assets/pensions, etc. But they all boil down to the idea that commercial life insurance is more efficient and flexible than the pension options.

There are some aspects surrounding the purchase of life insurance for pension maximization with which you must be very aware. Probably the biggest question is whether the life insurance is affordable and will remain that way for the entire life of the retiree. Almost by definition, the insurance must then be some form of permanent insurance. The amount of the insurance required is based upon some important assumptions. What will be the rate of return on the lump-sum payment? Is it a rate which can be guaranteed? What will future tax rates be? There are many issues to consider and questions to be answered before choosing pension maximization. Pension maximization has created some controversy because of unscrupulous insurance agents.

The real point we would like to end upon, is that the concept of pension maximization is neither good, nor bad. It is only the application of the concept, which makes the concept good or bad. It requires a full and exhaustive review and understanding of all the various elements discussed before it is applied. It is highly recommended by the authors that the concept be explored, but ensure that all the various nuances of your personal situation should be included, so as to make the best possible decision. We feel that the only way to get the right answer is to utilize the services of an unbiased advisor to help in the calculations. We know there are many good ethical insurance agents that would have your best interests at heart, but this decision is far too important. The fee you pay to obtain an unbiased opinion regarding this concept should pale to the ramifications on the rest of your life. Many "financial planners" eschew the concept completely, and that bias should also be considered. By exploring the concept, you should have a better understanding of your options, and you will be better prepared to make one of the most important financial decisions of your life.

Tentacle 2

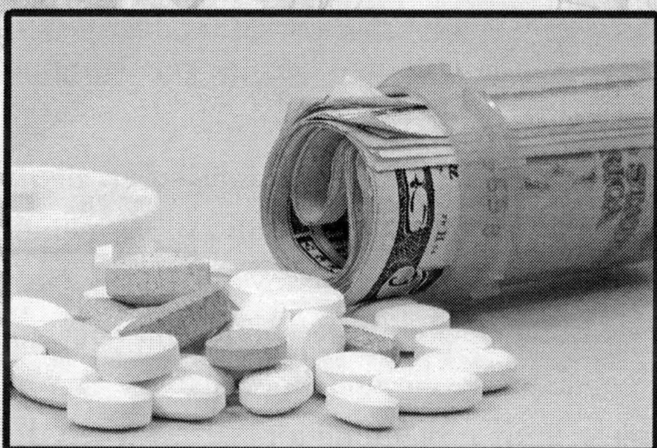

Social Security, Medicare & Medicaid

Tentacle 2

Social Security, Medicare, Medicaid

As we sat down to write this chapter, we felt the same as many of our clients feel when they face the task of signing up for Social Security and Medicare. They are confronted with so many bewildering rules and regulations that they don't know where to begin, or even whom to ask for help. Because everyone's situation is different, the government has adopted numerous rules and regulations in an attempt to encompass the subtleties of different situations. This has ultimately caused the system to become very complicated, and daunting to understand.

There is no way we could possibly cover all the various intricacies of the system, as that would surely require another whole book in and of itself. However, within this chapter, we will try to boil down all the volumes of rules into a clear and understandable set of guidelines that the vast majority of people can use in their planning for the day when they have to walk into the local Social Security office and sign up for their benefits.

Very few people know where the concept of Social Security began. In actuality, it is a German concept. Germany's Chancellor, Otto von Bismarck, decided he needed to come up with a program that he could give to his people. The goal was to make them grateful, and give them hope for a brighter future. The problem however, was that he really didn't want to have to pay for this program. Eventually becoming law in 1889, the system was craftily designed. You see when von Bismarck formed the original concept, he went to his actuaries, and asked them to tell him at what age would 95% of the general populace be dead. They studied the question, and reported back to him the age which they had determined. A brilliant strategist, he then told them to give him the age at which 95% of the surviving 5% would be dead. This way, he could offer a program, which virtually no one would ever collect upon. Once again the actuaries set about researching the question, ultimately reporting back with an answer. Based on their research, it was then determined that the age of 65 years would be the official age of retirement. That is the age at which the state would begin making old-age payments to surviving citizens. It was a brilliant plan, which would essentially cost nothing to implement. The program was widely hailed as a huge improvement in social programs, and proved a huge boon to the morale of the German population.

Fast forward 40 years, and Franklin D. Roosevelt was struggling with pulling the morale of our country from the depths of the Great Depression. He took a page from von Bismarck's playbook, and hit upon the concept of Social Security. What better way to give the country a vision of a bright and secure future. He went to his actuaries, and asked for an update of von Bismarck's studies. The actuaries went out and performed an exhaustive study of the same questions posed to von Bismarck's actuaries. Amazingly, the magic number came back exactly the same!!!

On August 14, 1935 President Franklin D. Roosevelt signed

the Social Security Act into law, and the first benefit payments began to be paid out in January 1940. There was a huge flaw in the study performed by the actuaries. The numbers were certainly exhaustive and far more accurate than the Germans' numbers. The problem with their research, was that the American actuaries failed to take into account the effect of a major World War, or the 1918 influenza pandemic. Combined, these major events caused the premature deaths of millions and millions of people worldwide. Throw in the benefits of technological and medical improvements, and it seems hard to believe that the actuaries believed that life expectancies had not improved over the previous 40 years.

So, the bottom line is, our system was founded upon some very bad assumptions right from the very beginning. In the early years of Social Security, just slightly more than 222,000 people were receiving monthly benefits. Today, one in seven Americans receives a monthly benefit. That equates to more than 42 million people. The number of people receiving benefits is one thing, but the truly alarming statistic is the ratio of workers paying into the system vs. recipients. In the early years, the ratio was roughly 42 workers to every recipient. Today the ratio has dropped to just over 3 workers for every recipient. With the coming swell of baby boomer retirements, the situation is bound to only get worse, as depicted in the following illustration;

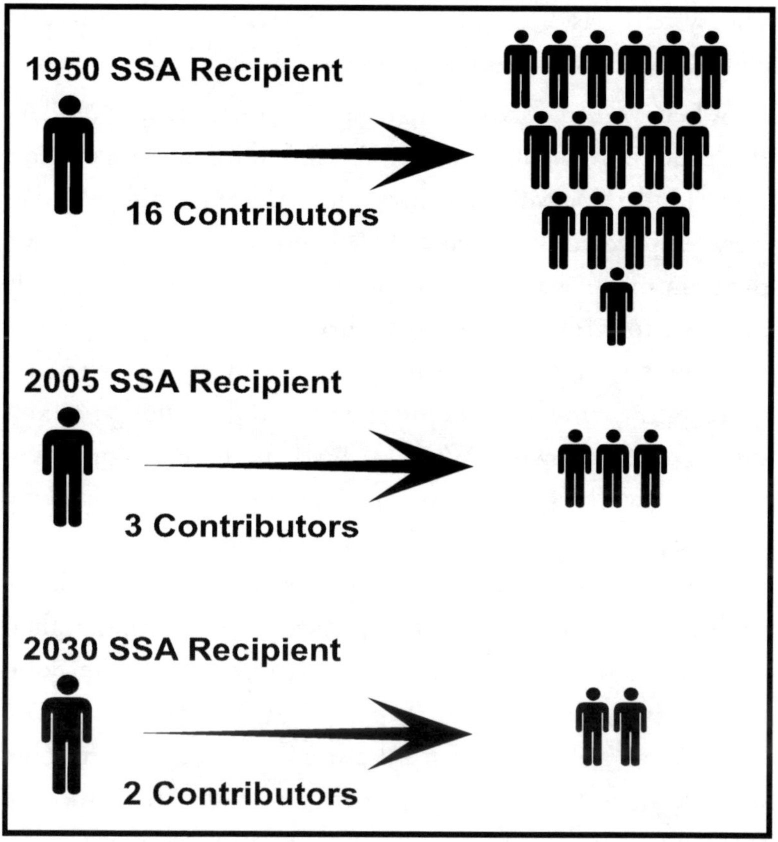

The above illustration was based on statistics from the Heritage Foundation, a research and educational institute. For more information, visit www.heritage.org.

Many people today are aware of the problems with the system, and have decided that there will be no Social Security system when they actually retire. Although certainly a possibility, we feel that the total elimination of all retirement and health benefits is a political decision which is just too far out of the mainstream to ever be a serious consideration. Lots of tinkering and changes will surely be affected in the future.

The system has been too entrenched within our society to consider wholesale elimination as a viable alternative.

When we first started drafting this document, President Bush had been making a lot of noise about his proposal to allow some kind of self-directed account. Although his proposals were attacked, and ultimately faded away, it seems to us that a program of this nature will be what the system will inevitably gravitate towards. Think of the private retirement system of our country, and you will understand why we make such a statement. Companies adopted pension and medical programs during and following World War II as an enticement for attracting workers. Soon, every major company was sponsoring lifetime pension programs, and healthcare insurance. However, as medical and technological improvements began to clearly improve life expectancies, companies began dumping their pensions, and adopting self-directed 401K's. This is a way for the company to shed their liability and shifting the onus of saving for retirement back to the worker. Today, the number of companies cutting back, or even eliminating their medical insurance programs is on the brink of causing a healthcare crisis. It is only a matter of time until the government comes to grips with the realities of the situation at hand, and institutes real reforms.

With all of that said, there is really no way of knowing what the future holds, so as planners we have to use the cards as we are dealt. We firmly believe that when the system is changed from it's current setup, there will probably be some kind of grandfathering of current participants that are over some age –

be it 45, 50 – whatever makes financial and political sense. So for the vast majority of you reading this book, we recommend assuming the system will essentially remain the same as it exists today – but keep a sharp ear tuned for changes.

The two major components of the Social Security Act of which we are concerned are Social Security (retirement income) and Medicare. We find that most people consider the two to be intertwined, when in reality, they are independent – even though both are administered by the Social Security Administration. So we'll address them separately.

The biggest question we find people asking, is, "When should I begin accepting retirement benefits?" First of all, everyone's situation is different, so there really is no simple answer. But there are some basics which helps make the answer to this question a little easier. For starters, any "insured" worker, age 62 or greater, is eligible to begin receiving income benefits. We used the term insured, because you become "insured" under the system once you have contributed to the system for 40 calendar quarters. Of course it's never as simple as that – but we'll assume most people have been working and contributing to the system for far longer than necessary to meet the minimum.

So why wouldn't you start taking free money at age 62? The answer is that it might not be free. If you continue to work and receive wages after age 62, there may be a penalty levied against the Social Security payments you receive. For every two dollars that you earn over and above an annually indexed limit, your benefit will be reduced by one dollar. The magic number for 2006 is $12,480. Think of it this way. If you continue to receive earned income of more than about $33,000, then even though you sign up to receive benefits, you will be penalized to the point where you really won't get the benefit. So why take it – defer taking the benefit until your earnings drop significantly, or you reach your full retirement age. That way you continue to earn credits, as well as increasing the monthly benefit you will receive in the future.

This brings us to another important concept that is part of your retirement benefit calculations. Full retirement age, is the age at which you are entitled to begin receiving 100% of your monthly benefit. That used to be 65 years of age for everyone, until 1983, when the current sliding scale of full retirement age was enacted. Today, full retirement age falls between 65 and 67, based upon you birth year. The Social Security Administration reports this information to you each year, on the annual estimate of benefits. This is the statement that you receive in the mail. Pay close attention to those statements. If there is an error, you have a limited amount of time to fix the error. You don't want to be shortchanged, due to an error.

Knowing your full retirement age is important. When you begin to receive benefits, for every month that you vary from that age, the amount of the benefit you receive is increased, or, decreased by a fixed percentage. If you begin receiving benefits before your full retirement age, the monthly payment amount is reduced. But, if you wait to begin receiving benefits until after full retirement age, your benefit amount is increased.

The last piece of the puzzle for most people is to understand that the earnings penalty is eliminated at your full retirement age. You can earn as much as you want, and there is no penalty applied against your benefit. Therefore, for the vast majority of Americans, it really makes no sense to defer taking your benefits after your full retirement age. Consequently, the decision of when to begin taking benefits usually boils down to "When do you intend to quit working?" If that's before your full retirement age, take it at age 62 or whenever you quit working, whichever is later. If you quit working after your full retirement age, take it at the full retirement age. Of course there are personal situations which may dictate other than this simple answer, but for the vast majority of people we've dealt with, this is by far the most common approach.

There is another whole set of rules regarding spousal benefits, but essentially the same concepts apply to spousal benefits as outlined above. A point of confusion for many people though, is over what a spouse is entitled to receive. The basic concept though, is that a spouse is entitled to either 50% of the other spouses benefit, or their own benefit – whichever is greater! Both spouses continue to collect his or her benefits until the death of the first spouse. At the first spouse's death, the surviving spouse is always entitled to the higher of the two benefits. For example, assume a wife is entitled to $1000 per month, and the husband is entitled to his own benefit of $800 per month. At the death of the first spouse, the surviving spouse would be entitled to the $1000 per month benefit. It matters not which spouse dies, the survivor will collect $1000 per month.

Once you've determined when to begin receiving your retirement benefit, the last piece is to sign up! You can, and should, sign up to receive benefits three months prior to the date you want to receive your first payment. This can actually be done via the mail, telephone, or by visiting one of the Social Security Administration's field offices. We generally recommend going to the office and applying in person, as that can speed the process by catching any irregularities right away. It may not be as convenient as using the mail or telephone, but a personal appointment can be time well spent. All that is required is to make an appointment at your local Social Security Administration office, and bring along evidence of your age. It is usually best to bring along a birth certificate, although there is a laundry list of other acceptable documents. That's it! Enjoy your benefit!

Medicare is simple to figure out when to sign up for coverage, but beyond that, it's benefits are tough to come to grips with. If signing up for benefits were linked to Social Security retirement benefits, it would be somewhat easy to figure out when to apply for benefits. But it is a completely different system of benefits, and that's where most Americans get it wrong. Even though you apply for Medicare benefits via the Social Security Administration, the program is administered by the Centers for Medicare & Medicaid Services, which is within the Department of Health and Human Services.

Medicare is really comprised of four parts – A, B, C and D. Part A is what we all know as hospitalization, but it actually covers in-patient hospital care, post-hospital home health care, skilled nursing home care, and in some instances hospice care. Part B is a voluntary program, meaning there is a cost to have it.

Part B covers physicians' services, out-patient hospital services, and a host of other non-institutional services. Part C is where Medicare can contract with HMOs, PPOs, and other plans – allowing for managed care options. And lastly, Part D is the much ballyhooed, voluntary prescription drug program, which went into effect in January 2006.

It is not our intent here to focus on the specifics of the benefits provided under each of the parts of Medicare. There are plenty of other great sources which can be accessed to get the details. Rather, we'd like to focus on when to enroll, and what parts to consider.

All people that are age 65 and over, that are entitled to receive Social Security retirement benefits (whether they actually started taking them or not), are eligible for Part A benefits. They can receive those benefits regardless of whether they are working. Enrollment does not affect, in any way, their Social Security benefits. It's important to note, with only limited exceptions, in order to qualify for benefits, you must be age 65 or over. So just because one spouse is over 65 – does not mean the other spouse qualifies for coverage. Each person must be age 65 or over. By the way, there is no monthly premium for Part A coverage, so it makes all the sense in the world to sign up for benefits at age 65.

Any person eligible for Part A coverage is entitled to participate in Part B. Even if you do not qualify for Part A, and meet certain criteria, you can purchase Part B coverage. Part B is not free, and is therefore a voluntary benefit. When you enroll for Part A, you will automatically be enrolled for Part

B, unless you elect not to enroll at that time. It is important to understand that there is a timeframe for eligibility, which begins on the first of the month, three months prior to your 65th birthday, and ends on the last day of the month, three months after your birth date. This period of time is your initial enrollment period. Coverage begins during the month you turn 65, or the first of the month following your enrollment. If, for whatever reason, you miss the initial enrollment dates, there is always the ability to enroll during the general enrollment period, which runs from January 1st to March 31st of each year. The catch though, is that coverage for someone who enrolls during the general enrollment period does not begin until the following July 1st. If you fail to enroll during your initial, or special enrollment period (outlined below), there is higher premium charged to those individuals, essentially 10% additional charge per month for each year that they fail to enroll. So, the general rule of thumb is to enroll during your initial enrollment period.

There is one major exception to our rule of thumb however. That exception involves people that, because of employment, continue to be covered under a group health plan after attaining age 65. There is a special enrollment period, which extends seven months from the point when the group coverage provided by your employer ends. Because there is a monthly premium for coverage under Part B, it may make sense to just continue your group coverage until you quit working, and pick up the Part B at that time.

Part B, as well as Part A have all kinds of rules regarding

what is and isn't covered, co-insurances, deductibles, and benefit limits. Once again, there are numerous sources of good information regarding these details. Probably the best source of good information is the government's own web site at www.ssa.gov.

Part C represents an interesting alternative to Part A and B. It is essentially a contract between Medicare and private organizations, which make managed care programs available to eligible Part A and B participants. In essence, it is really as simple as deciding whether you want a traditional fee-for-service plan (Part A and B) or a managed care program (Part C). Of course, the monthly premium charge to be in a Part C program is not necessarily the same as the monthly premium for Part B. The bottom line is – do your homework ahead of time. Research what options exist in your area, and compare the benefits provided by the Part C program with the standard benefits of Part A and B.

Lastly, and quite possibly the most inconsequential, at least in its' current form, is Part D. This is the new prescription drug benefit. In 2005 the benefit was merely a drug discount card, which was projected to offer discounts from 10% to 25%. The "real" benefit began in January 2006. Although a huge improvement over past prescription benefits – essentially nothing – the new Part D benefit is marginal at best. To enroll in the program is voluntary. What most people don't understand is that Part D can only be purchased from private insurers. It is not like Part B, where the premium is paid to the government via a reduction from your Social Security check. The premium charged is much like Part B, meaning if you don't enroll when you are first eligible, there will probably be a late enrollment penalty to get into the program. The government established a model program, which must be offered by the private insurer, but it also allows the insurer to come up with plans of their own design as well. So there exists a broad spectrum of plans

Part D

Prescription Drug Expense	**Beneficiary Cost**	**Plan Pays**
First $250	100% (up to $250)	Nothing
$251 to $2,250	25% (up to $500)	75% (up to $1,500)
$2,251 to $5,100	100%	Nothing
$5,100 and over	Up to 5% (income tested)	95% or more

and costs. The government model plan is as follows:

Some quick calculations on the above table shows that the average plan participant will pay about $4020 (beneficiary cost plus expected premium) out of their own pockets to cover $5000 of prescription drugs. Of course, the real benefit of this program kicks in after you incur more than $5100 of expenses.

Since this benefit is brand new, and a major political accomplishment, we expect that Congress will tinker with the structure of this program for years to come. The best advice we can offer is to shop around among the plans available, pay close attention to what happens in Congress, and react accordingly.

Although not officially a part of the Social Security/Medicare program, Medigap insurance is absolutely an important part of the system, so much so in fact, that the government got into the act by mandating a formal structure of policy designs which could be offered by private insurance companies.

Essentially, Medigap policies are all designed to cover beneficiary costs which are not covered by Medicare. Prior to the government's involvement, there were a huge and often confusing array of choices available to Medicare beneficiaries. Now, the policies are standardized, and represent several distinct policies, each providing different levels of benefit. There are also two additional options available, which are identical to two of the "pricier" options, but with a higher deductible, which is indexed to the Consumer Price Index for urban consumers.

Although we will not list all the details of each of the different plans, it is extremely important to do your homework on these plans. The government assigns letters to these policies, i.e. Plan A, B, etc., but insurance companies can call them whatever they want, as long as they conform to the mandated benefits of the government Plans. There is no mandated cost, so even though the benefits are identical, companies are free to charge whatever they want. As always, the devil is in the details, so you must be extremely vigilant to ensure you are getting what you want. We highly recommend you enlist the assistance of a professional to help in understanding all the nuances of the broad list of options available to you.

Once you've made your decision to purchase a Medigap policy, it is important to realize there is an open enrollment period, which guarantees that you cannot be denied Medigap insurance, or charged a higher premium because of health problems. This is only true during the eligibility period of six months immediately following the effective date of enrolling in Medicare Part B. Although you are guaranteed coverage if you enroll during this period, there may still be a "pre-existing conditions" clause within the policy. If a policy contains this clause, it can only limit benefits because of the clause during the first six months. Once again, not all policies contain such clauses, so do your homework. The bottom line is if you fail to enroll during the guaranteed enrollment period, insurers are free to deny coverage or offer only those policies they want to offer.

Retirement entails a lot of decisions, especially when it comes to Social Security and Medicare. For most of us, it happens all at once, and we are under the gun to make all the myriad of major life altering decisions within a very short timeframe. Although the process may seem daunting, a little bit of pre-planning and research can make the process go smooth and seamless. Don't allow all the minutiae of details to bog you down in the decision process. Gaining an understanding of the big picture, and how all the pieces fit together to provide a safe and secure retirement is the way to make good strategic decisions. If you enter the process armed with a little knowledge and enthusiasm, then the octopus will pose no threat.

Tentacle 5

Retirement & Income Taxes

Tentacle 3
Retirement & Income Taxes

Taxes seem to be everyone's favorite topic, especially in March and April. Unfortunately, it is rarely a happy topic for most people. We've never met anyone that wanted our assistance in figuring out how to pay more taxes. We often tell our clients that our job is really to cause you to pay more taxes, not less. If they don't want that type of situation, then we can readily introduce them to lots of brokers that will help them generate capital losses, which they can use to reduce their taxes. When you look at taxes from that perspective, owing more taxes is really a good thing! Never, ever, allow the tax tail to wag the dog. When this occurs, the person ends up losing financially. Unfortunately, many tax scams prey upon those that have the desire to avoid taxes. Ultimately, an unwise or ill-advised choice could result in serious legal fees and horrible consequences. It is our constitutional right to minimize the taxes we pay, but illegal to evade taxes. The gray area between the two extremes is usually where people can get into trouble

Obviously, we are being overly simplistic. A large part of the planning that we do for clients involves minimizing the effect of taxes on their lifestyles. Understanding how our tax system works is really the key to minimizing your contribution to Uncle Sam. Good retirement tax planning needs to be a coordinated effort, and requires a full understanding of the tax consequences of each and every asset that you own. Each type of asset has its own unique tax ramifications, and many assets have varying consequences to your tax liability. It is only through planning and knowledge, that an effective tax strategy can be employed.

We have found very little in the way of good overall planning guidance. The help that is available focuses on the tax ramifications of individual products, such as IRA's, Roth IRA's, 401K rollovers, annuities, etc., etc., etc. All too often, a sales person will offer tax guidance by explaining why his or her product is the solution to every problem you've ever imagined, including world hunger. Although the "product du jour" may sometimes actually work, we believe that such an approach to tax planning is oftentimes driven more by the desire for commission, than the desire to help improve someone's lifestyle. Once again, it is absolutely imperative to understand all of a person's goals and aspirations before you can properly understand the full ramifications of a tax decision. Individual products should be considered as individual tools in the carpenter's toolbox, not the blueprint for the house. Understanding and mastering the use of a tool is important, but without the blueprint, will you get the design you wanted?

First, you should understand, there is no silver bullet that solves all tax issues, and rescues everyone from paying taxes. Each and every individual's tax situation is unique. It is much more important to understand what it is you want to achieve, than to figure out how to do it. We often ask audiences: "How do you get to Chicago?" The correct answer could be many different things, north, south, plane, boat, etc., etc., etc., but only depending on your starting point. You see, how to do it is not the important part of the question. The unspoken, vital, part of the question is what your starting point is, and, do you even want to go to Chicago? Most of the people we encounter, don't really want to reduce the taxes they pay to the government. They just want more disposable dollars in their own pockets. Tax reduction is just a means to achieving their financial goals.

We believe the product approach to resolving tax issues is rarely appropriate. By way of example, I would like to present a scenario, and contrast the product approach versus the planning approach. A retired person came to us, complaining about paying too much in taxes. She wanted to figure out how to pay less to the federal government. This individual is widowed, collecting Social Security, with a small pension, and has investment assets generating taxable interest (most commonly CDs). Below is a representation of her 2003 federal tax return. The actual year not as important as the concept:

Taxable Interest:	$ 16,000
Pension	$ 20,000
Social Security Benefits:	$ 14,000
Adjusted Gross Income:	$ 47,900
Federal Taxes Due:	$ 6,554

The product solution generally comes in two forms – she should purchase annuities or tax exempt municipal bonds. Let's look at what happens with both approaches, and see why they may or may not be appropriate.

First, the tax exempt bonds will affect the tax return in an interesting manner. The interest she receives is definitely income tax-free, but this product solution does not address the impact that the interest income has upon the taxability of Social Security benefits. You see, the calculations used to determine the taxability of her Social Security benefits depend upon a couple of things, including whether or not she has tax exempt income! In this example, the overall tax is indeed reduced, but because the tax exempt income is included in the calculation of the taxability of Social Security, her Social Security income is still subject to higher taxes. Let's look at her calculations now:

	Before Bonds	**With Bonds**
Taxable Interest	$ 16,000	$ 0
Tax-Free Interest	$ 0	$ 16,000
Pension	$ 20,000	$ 20,000
Social Security Benefits:	$ 14,000	$ 14,000
Adjusted Gross Income:	$ 47,900	$ 31,900
Federal Taxes Due:	$ 6,554	$ 3,096

This is certainly a very nice improvement in the lifestyle of this individual, actually reducing her tax liability to about half the prior amount. But could it be better? This is where the annuity salesman comes along, and claims superiority. Remember, the tax exempt interest causes her Social Security income to be taxed at a higher rate. The annuity transforms the income into tax-deferred income, and results in the following changes to our client's tax return:

	Before Bonds	With Bonds	With Annuity
Taxable Interest	$ 16,000	$ 0	$ 0
Tax-Free Interest	$ 0	$ 16,000	$ 0
Pension	$ 20,000	$ 20,000	$ 20,000
Social Security Benefits:	$ 14,000	$ 14,000	$ 14,000
Adjusted Gross Income:	$ 47,900	$ 31,900	$ 21,000
Federal Taxes Due:	$ 6,554	$ 3,096	$ 1,461

Notice, we've managed to reduce the federal tax liability even further. It is now about half the tax liability of the tax exempt income example. We must ask the question: Is this a superior solution?

The pundits of each approach proudly claim superiority, and make convincing arguments for their respective approach. The financial press is all too often black and white on these issues, meaning they tend to profess to be experts, and ultimately proclaim one solution is better than the other. In reality, once again, the wrong question is being posed. Remember, there are many different ways to get to Chicago! However, do you really want to go to Chicago? Or, in this situation, do you really want to reduce federal taxes?

If the client's goal is to merely reduce taxes paid to the federal government, clearly the annuity solution is better than tax exempt bonds. But what is the rest of the story? Does the individual need the income today? Tax deferral means, by definition, that you do not take income today. Does she desire to leave a full inheritance to her children? Tax deferral only defers the taxation. Ultimately, the beneficiaries will pay the full ordinary taxes on the annuity. Is she comfortable with tax exempt bonds/bond funds? Some people cannot sleep at night unless they have FDIC insurance. Does she have philanthropic or charitable intentions? Some would argue that better tax results could be achieved by utilizing various charitable gifting techniques.

The point we want to make, is that there is no one right solution to this situation. A proper solution requires a total understanding of the individual's situation, and more importantly their real desires. The knee-jerk product solution is the product purveyor's justification for an easy sale. Only through the planning process can the total ramifications and end results of tax planning be coordinated to accomplish the clients' ultimate goals.

I am certain you have heard, at one time or other, that the way to plan for a successful and comfortable retirement, is to accumulate a large enough pile of money. The pile is large enough to enable us to take a conservative withdrawal rate (4 to 6%) from the principal to meet our spending needs – and ultimately never touch the principal. Put another way, it says, ***live off the interest, and never touch the principal!!!*** If you can do that, you can probably plan on living to a ripe old age and never need be concerned about running out of money. Many people believe in this age-old guideline\rule of thumb. We feel it is imperative to dispel this great myth. The basic concept of the myth is great, until you consider its tax ramifications. Let me first state, this approach may possibly work. The problem is the pile of money required to generate the needed income, has gotten far too large for most people. Neglecting the tax ramifications of this approach makes the problem even bigger. We actually alluded to the problem in the previous example.

To illustrate, let's look at a typical retirement calculation. If someone wanted to live on $50,000 per year from their investments, and was comfortable with a withdrawal rate of 5%, then the simplistic answer that the financial press gives them is that they need to accumulate $1 Million dollars ($1M times 5% = $50,000). This is pure bunk, and should be considered a serious violation of ethics. This approach totally ignores the effect of taxes, as well as inflation.

In the first year, this individual would only have about $40 to $45 thousand dollars to live on, not the $50,000 they wanted, due to federal taxes. Of course, this assumes we are talking about an accumulation in some kind of qualified account. That is the only place where most Americans manage to save sizeable amounts. Next, compound inflation out a few years, and these people have a greatly reduced lifestyle, due to the fixed income ($50,000) being generated. So, to fix the problem and manage the effects of inflation on their lifestyle, we have to make the savings accumulation much larger. As their income now increases, presumably keeping pace with inflation, now their tax liability is presumed to also increase, therefore causing the need for an even greater accumulation of principal. Now, assuming a long retirement, and only modest inflation as well as modest tax rates, the original pile of money required to maintain their current lifestyle has perhaps doubled. The pile has now become a great mountain.

Unfortunately, the reality is that very few people have managed to save and put away enough to satisfy the amount required by this type of calculation. To save a greater amount of money for retirement is too often an unrealistic goal. What can be done?

I go back to the planning approach. Let's dispel the basic assumption of the simplistic approach to retirement accumulations. The myth must die! Take traditional wisdom and turn it on its head. By this, I mean let's not live off the interest of our principal, and save the principal. ***Rather, we should be planning on living off the principal and saving the interest!!*** You see, the federal government wants us to live off the interest, because they get to tax it! **Interest is taxable as ordinary income.** ***However, if we spend our principal, there are zero taxes to pay.*** $50,000 of taxable interest income is entirely different than $50,000 principal, when it comes to your lifestyle!

Let us walk you through an actual example, because this is such an important tax planning concept. Although this example involves a product solution, the concept is the important thing to grasp.

Let's assume a couple with the following 2003 federal tax return:

Taxable interest:	$ 15,000
Ordinary Dividends:	$ 3,500
Tax Free Interest:	$ 0

Pension:	$ 48,000
Social Security Benefits:	$ 23,000
Adjusted Gross Income:	$ 86,050
Taxable Income:	$ 68,550
Federal Taxes Due:	$ 10,639

The taxable interest ($15,000) is being generated by $500,000 worth of Certificates of Deposit, averaging 3% interest. They are employing the typical approach to income planning, namely living off the interest generated by the CDs. They need that extra $15,000 to maintain their standard of living.

We would suggest a different tactic. They could redeploy the dollars to two different annuities. One of them would be a traditional deferred annuity, and the other would be an immediate annuity with a five-year payout. The deferred annuity will contain $427,368 and the immediate annuity would hold $72,632. We are going to assume the annuities will be paying 1% more in interest than the CDs (CD @ 3% and annuity @4%). This is generally the typical spread on high quality annuities over CD rates. The spread between the two products generally remain the same, as rates rise or fall. Let us explain why we need two annuities, as well as the reason for the different amounts.

The immediate annuity will start producing $1,250 per month of income ($15,000 per year) to the couple, based on an actual quote in the fall of 2004. That is the same amount that the CDs generated, so there is no reduction in the couple's disposable income.

At this point, you may be confused or dismayed. How can an annuity with only $72,632 produce as much income as $500,000 in CDs? No insurance company is paying that high of an interest rate. If they are, then they will soon go out of business! The key to understanding how this happens, is to look at the cash flow. Income is not the same as interest!!!!! The CDs are generating interest income, which is 100% taxable at ordinary income rates. The annuity is generating income, but only 15% of it is taxable at ordinary rates. You see, with each monthly income check the insurance company sends you, they are sending you interest, as well as a return of your principal! The interest represents only about 15% of each payment, and that is the amount that is taxable – the principal that is being returned to you is tax-free!!! Of the $1250 monthly check you receive, approximately $1037.50 is your original deposit, and $212.50 is the interest. Let's look at the difference this would make to this couple's tax situation.

Taxable Interest:	$ 2,550
Ordinary Dividends:	$ 3,500
Tax-Free Interest:	$ 0
Pension:	$ 48,000
Social Security Benefits:	$ 23,000
Adjusted Gross Income:	$ 73,300
Taxable Income:	$ 55,880
Federal Taxes Due:	$ 7,549

What a difference! They save $ 3,110 per year in federal taxes (and probably more each successive year). That savings could fund a nice vacation, dinners out, tanks of gas, etc.

But we need to answer a couple more questions that are hopefully lurking in the back of your mind. What happens at the end of the five years? Well, since the immediate annuity is returning the principal to you over the five years, when that time frame is complete, your money is gone!!!!! That $72,632 is completely spent. One might suggest that this is a horrible planning technique. Although the CDs cost us more in taxation, we haven't spent the principal.

This is a good time to introduce the traditional annuity. That $427,368 we put in the second annuity has never been touched. The original $427,368 has now grown to $519,958 over the five years that we were drawing from the immediate annuity. You see, we were saving the interest, while spending our principal!!!!!!

Compare the two approaches and see which is more effective. With the traditional approach of living off interest only, at the end of the five years, we have $500,000 in the bank. With the opposite approach, living off the principal, we have $519,958 at the end of the five years, and we have also enjoyed the use of an additional $3,110 each and every year for the five years – which is the tax savings.

Yes – we can hear the skeptics already. You may be thinking, "Now what – I've managed to save money each year for five years, but now I've got a bigger tax problem at the end of the five years." Remember, as we said earlier, tax deferral means you owe taxes later – it does not make them disappear.

First of all, there is no magic to the five year number. We used it for simplicity's sake in this example. In real life, you would probably plan for a much longer term of years – 10, 15 or 20 years, whatever fits your personal situation. Secondly, even if you had executed the strategy as shown above, at the end of the five years, just go ahead and execute the strategy again. Split the remaining annuity into two, and start taking an income from the smaller one over another fixed term (five years). Keep in mind, the tax results will not be quite as nice as the first time. The IRS will require you to start taking some of the deferred interest from the new immediate annuity. This should not be a cause for alarm though, as the new monthly payment might now be, say, 70% tax-free return of principal instead of 85%. It still beats 100% taxable as a CD.

We should explain a couple of quick caveats regarding this strategy. First and foremost, this strategy only works with non-qualified monies (funds which have not been previously invested in a tax-deferred account). It will not help with IRAs, 401K's, or any other qualified monies, as they are generally 100% taxable distributions, no matter what type of investment they happen to be sitting in prior to the distribution. Secondly, insurance company solvency, and the annuity liquidity can be an issue. As for company solvency, a little homework, and due diligence is certainly in order. There are however, many high quality, financially sound companies available. The insurance industry is also proud to point out that they have never allowed policyholders of an insolvent company, to lose their money – meaning that some company has always stepped in to rescue the insolvent company. That does not however mean that policyholders got their money right away. In fact, they may have had to wait years to get it. But the little known fact, is that the same may hold true for banks. FDIC does not guarantee a speedy return of your principal, just a return of it. Many of the victims of the early 1990s Savings and Loan crisis had to wait a long time for their money to be returned.

Lastly, the liquidity issue of the annuities should be addressed. There are many annuities that are available from many different companies. Some are good, some are bad, and there are a slew of them somewhere between the two extremes. There are also lots of different bells and whistles that are available on these annuities. Liquidity of the annuity is often a function of the term of the contract, as well as the bells and whistles. All we can say, is, do your homework and read the fine print. If you are not totally comfortable with "legalese," you should probably utilize a planner that is well-versed in the contracts and the fine print.

We will conclude by saying that liquidity should not be a major concern. Remember, we have been talking about an alternative to the traditional approach to retirement planning – live off the interest and never touch the principal. If you are not planning on touching the principal, it does not matter if the principal is not totally liquid.

Once again, please do not construe this strategy as the magic silver bullet to everyone's tax planning issues. It works nicely in the proper scenario, but could also be a disaster in another person's situation. It is only through a thorough analysis of the big picture, that a proper tactic can be developed and employed.

In wrapping up this chapter, we've hopefully given you some food for thought, and tried to dispel some of bogus advice all too common in the popular financial press. We can't overemphasize the need to look beyond the typical knee-jerk, product-oriented solutions that the major financial institutions advertise as the mecca of retirement planning. Their slogans might sound like they care about you, but the bottom-line is often their bottom line. The multiple intricacies affecting your tax situation are too interconnected to rely upon a single product to solve your problems. We suggest that you consult a highly qualified, independent planner that will ask the right questions and is interested in your true goals and ambitions. We believe this is the only way to develop a plan of attack to tackle taxes and retirement income.

Tentacle 4

Maintaining Lifestyle Without Outliving Income

Tentacle 4
Maintaining Lifestyle & Not Outliving Income

This chapter addresses a problem that could be the single biggest retirement mistake that people make…failing to plan for a long life. As silly as that may sound, it is a very common error. This mistake can often have severe negative repercussions because once made, it is very hard to undo.

Unfortunately, some people are not aware that they have failed to properly plan for their longevity until they have already been retired for many years. As the retirement years pass, the cost of living rises; and they slowly begin to realize that their plan is not allowing them to maintain the same lifestyle they had in the beginning. Unfortunately, at this point, there are few options available to them, especially since re-entering the work force at age 70 or 80 is, in most instances, neither desirable, nor realistic. When this occurs, many retirees are forced to attempt to restructure their investments to earn higher rates of return, which means exposing themselves to more risk. Of course, retirement is not the time most people should be exposing themselves to higher financial risks. Unfortunately, their only other alternative is to reduce their living expenses. For obvious reasons, this is not a situation that anyone ever wants to experience.

Life Expectancy

Although it is impossible to predict the length of anyone's life, many pre-retirees forget the fact that people in general are living much longer, especially with the rapid advances in medical science and technology. Many people find it difficult to imagine themselves living into their 80s, 90s, or past the age of 100. Once in a while, we will have clients tell us that they come from strong stock and have a family history of longevity, but most of the time clients will laugh and joke that they will never make it past 80 years of age. Problems arise when their financial plan reflects this assumption, but then they live much longer than they anticipated. At this critical time, retirees begin to outlive their assets and leave themselves with few options.

Inflation

Failing to consider inflation costs is the second common mistake made when planning for retirement. Many Americans retiring today rely on pension plans as their primary source of income. Since most pension plans provide a fixed stream of income, they do not increase as the cost of living increases (inflation). Social Security is the next largest income source for many retirees. Although Social Security currently carries a cost of living adjustment, most benefit amounts are not substantial enough to provide enough of an increase to keep up with the overall rise in household budget costs. As a result, far too many retirees find themselves dependent on a fixed income for ten, twenty, or thirty years. Consequently, their income buys less and less as time goes on. This means that retirees buy fewer bags of groceries, dine out less, and may become unable to pay certain bills. In short, their standard of living decreases.

This problem calls for a shift in how we all view risk. When many people hear the word risk, they automatically think of stock market losses. Their perception is that they would never want to put their retirement dollars at risk in the markets because they could lose that money. While it is true that the stock market involves risk, there is also a risk factor in NOT having a portion of your money invested in stocks because your assets may not outpace inflation. If this occurs, you run the risk of having your standard of living decrease throughout your retirement. Worse yet, you may completely deplete your assets and still have many years to live. For this reason, a sufficient retirement plan must focus on MAINTAINING LIFESTYLE even during periods of inflation.

In a perfect world, we could all just cash in our investments at retirement, put them in guaranteed bonds or CD's, and live off of the interest until the end of our lives. While some retirees have accumulated enough money to do this, most have not. That is, most Americans today just do not have enough retirement assets to park them in fixed investments that do not outpace the costs of inflation. While those investments seem quite safe on the surface, they can be a silent killer of a comfortable retirement. As a result, most of today's retirees must plan to keep a percentage of their money invested for growth; having their assets work just as hard for them during retirement as they did while they were saving for their retirement nest egg. We will say it again; a good retirement plan MUST outpace inflation and prepare for realistic time horizons. For these reasons, managing risk and taxation become critical elements in the financial planning process.

So how do you plan for more than 30 years of retirement?

There are two widely accepted formulas for helping to ensure that you retire with assets that are sufficient enough to outpace inflation and maintain your lifestyle. One is called Preservation of Principal. With this model, you strive to build a nest egg that is large enough so you can live using only the return on your investments. Therefore, you will never touch the actual principal. For instance, if you have a savings of two million dollars, you could safely assume that you can draw an income of five percent per year, or $100,000. The problems with Preservation of Principal are that it often requires a large sum of money in order to live off of interest alone, and that challenge becomes greater and greater as inflation increases your cost of living. As we have mentioned before, few people can actually end up building up this amount of savings. Because of this fact, the second formula, Liquidation of Principal, will better meet the needs of most people. With this concept, you draw interest and principal. As a result, a smaller sum will provide the same income for a certain time period. The question becomes; for how long of a time period do you plan? Since you do not know how long you will live, the Liquidation of Principal calculations should be computed using very conservative assumptions of high inflation, high taxes, modest returns, and long life expectancy. Because of the many variables involved, these calculations can be rather complicated. Therefore, this is an area that you should carefully focus on when designing your financial plan.

So, how should a person go about this task and what factors must be considered? Let's begin by looking at some historical consumer price index (CPI) numbers. **Illustration A1** shows the CPI year by year going back to 1965. As you can see, the actual year by year rate of inflation fluctuates greatly. As a result, you need to ask yourself which average rate of return you are comfortable using for your financial planning. This variable should be watched carefully and re-addressed periodically as trends change.

Illustration A1

History of Inflation

CPI Annual % Increase 1965 to 2004

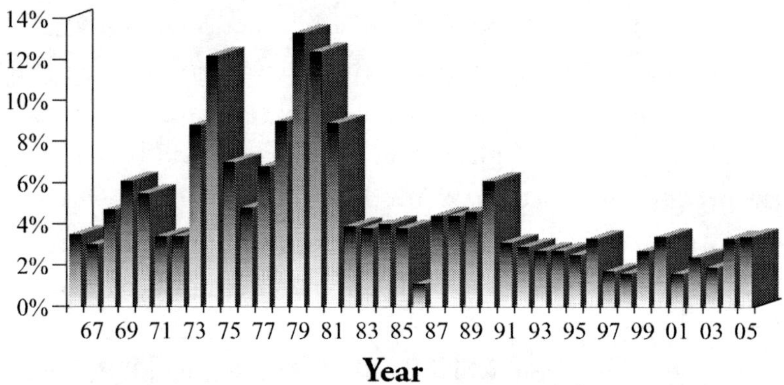

The above illustration was created and provided by Financial Profiles, Inc.

Illustration A2 shows the average CPI increase during each decade since 1970. You will see that we have recently enjoyed relatively low inflation rates compared to the 1970s and 1980s. During the last 40 years, the overall average CPI is 4.7%, although we have averaged less than 3% since 1990.

Illustration A2

Inflation-Decades in Review

		Annual Average CPI Increase
The 70s	1970-1979	7.4%
The 80s	1980-1989	5.1%
The 90s	1990-1999	2.9%
The 2000s	2000-2005	2.7%
Last 40 Years	1966-2005	4.7%

Source: Bureau of Labor Statistics. Consumer Price Index (CPI-U).
Data through year end 2005
The above illustration was created and provided by Financial Profiles, Inc.

When working with our clientele, we usually assume at least a 4% cost of living adjustment per year as we plan cash flow and distributions.

The next thing that needs to be addressed along with inflation is life expectancy. **Illustration A3** shows current life expectancy statistics obtained from the Office of the Chief Actuary, Social Security Administration (July 2003). As you can see, a male retiring at age 60 has a statistical average life expectancy of almost twenty years while a 60-year-old female has almost 23 years. A 65-year-old male can expect to live at least another 15 years and a 70-year-old male at least another 12 years. Keep in mind these are statistical averages, which means it is possible that these numbers could be low estimates for you! Also, remember that the life expectancy tables are trending upwards. In other words, on average, we are living longer. As life expectancy figures continue to rise, it will not be uncommon for many Americans to have retirements that last longer than their working careers. With the amazing advances in medical science, there is every reason to believe that these trends will continue. Therefore, we must plan for a retirement that will last 30 years or more.

Illustration A3

Life Expectancy Table

Life Expectancy in Years

Age	Male	Female	Age	Male	Female	Age	Male	Female
0	73.9	79.2	25	50.4	55.2	50	27.6	31.6
1	73.5	78.8	26	49.4	54.3	51	26.8	30.7
2	72.5	77.8	27	48.5	53.3	52	25.9	29.8
3	71.6	76.8	28	47.6	52.3	53	25.1	28.9
4	70.6	75.9	29	46.6	51.3	54	24.2	28.0
5	69.6	74.9	30	45.7	50.4	55	23.4	27.1
6	68.6	73.9	31	44.7	49.4	56	22.6	26.3
7	67.6	72.9	32	43.8	48.4	57	21.8	25.4
8	66.6	71.9	33	42.9	47.5	58	21.0	24.6
9	65.7	70.9	34	41.9	46.5	59	20.3	23.7
10	64.7	69.9	35	41.0	45.6	60	19.5	22.9
11	63.7	68.9	36	40.1	44.6	61	18.7	22.1
12	62.7	67.9	37	39.1	43.6	62	18.0	21.3
13	61.7	66.9	38	38.2	42.7	63	17.3	20.5
14	60.7	66.0	39	37.3	41.7	64	16.5	19.7
15	59.7	65.0	40	36.4	40.8	65	15.8	18.9
16	58.8	64.0	41	35.5	39.9	66	15.2	18.2
17	57.8	63.0	42	34.6	38.9	67	14.5	17.4
18	56.9	62.0	43	33.7	38.0	68	13.9	16.7
19	55.9	61.1	44	32.1	37.1	69	13.2	16.0
20	55.0	60.1	45	31.9	36.1	70	12.6	15.3
21	54.1	59.1	46	31.0	35.2	71	12.0	14.6
22	53.2	58.2	47	30.2	34.3	72	11.4	13.9
23	52.2	57.2	48	29.3	33.4	73	10.8	13.2
24	51.3	56.2	49	28.5	32.5	74	10.3	12.6

Illustration A3-(*Continued*)

Life Expectancy Table-(*Continued*)

Life Expectancy in Years

Age	Male	Female
75	9.7	11.9
76	9.2	11.3
77	8.7	10.7
78	8.2	10.1

Age	Male	Female
79	7.7	9.5
80	7.2	8.9
81	6.8	8.4
82	6.4	7.9

Age	Male	Female
83	5.9	7.3
84	5.6	6.9
85	5.2	6.4

Source: Office of the Chief Actuary, Social Security Administration (July 2003)
The above illustration was created and provided by Financial Profiles, Inc.

When considering these two realities, inflation and life expectancy, you realize that your planned cash flow needs to increase each year to maintain your buying power, which translates into maintaining your standard of living. Furthermore, you need to plan for your increased cash flow needs beyond your reasonable life expectancy. Why beyond reasonable life expectancy you may ask? Because it would be a bittersweet situation if the funds in your financial plan are depleted by the age you figured that you would have passed on, but instead you are still alive and kicking. Nature might surprise you by giving you a few extra decades of long life. Those additional years will still involve bags of groceries, utilities, housing, medical care, and a host of other expenses, all ticking upwards at the rate of inflation.

Let's put some real numbers into this scenario. Let's look at the example of Fred, a 65-year-old retiring in 2005 with an annual financial need of $36,000. That means that after all taxes are paid, Fred estimates that he needs $3,000 per month for living expenses. This scenario is shown in **Illustration A4**.

Using a 4% assumption of inflation, Fred will need a yearly income of $43,800 ($3,650 per month) at age 70; $53,289 ($4,441 per month) at age 75; and by the time he reaches 80 he will need $64,834 ($5,403 per month) just to enjoy the same standard of living as when he began retirement. By age 87, Fred's income needs have more than doubled from his initial retirement date.

Illustration A4

Age	Total Annual Income Needed	Age	Total Annual Income Needed	Age	Total Annual Income Needed
65	$36,000	77	$57,637	89	$92,279
66	37,440	78	59,943	90	95,970
67	38,938	79	62,340	91	99,809
68	40,495	80	64,834	92	103,801
69	42,115	81	67,427	93	107,953
70	43,800	82	70,124	94	112,271
71	45,551	83	72,929	95	116,762
72	47,374	84	75,847	96	121,433
73	49,268	85	78,880	97	126,290
74	51,239	86	82,036	98	131,342
75	53,289	87	85,317	99	136,595
76	55,420	88	88,730		

The above illustration was created and provided by Financial Profiles, Inc.

Now, imagine that our retiree started with an income stream consisting of a fixed pension and Social Security, providing him with an annual income of $43,020 after taxes. This income would increase slightly each year, due to assumed cost of living increases in the Social Security benefit. This is shown on the first line of the Summary Timeline under "Total Annual Income Sources." At first, these two income streams would have provided for his needs quite nicely. But by the time he reached 70, he was living to his means, and by age 71 his income streams were below his needs. When this occurs, he better have assets to make up the difference, or his only other option is to reduce his living expenses. Fred would be running a shortage of $6,500 a year at age 75, and by the time he reached age 87 he would be running an annual shortage of more than $32,000. In Fred's case, his standard of living would have been cut in half during his retirement. A loss of that amount could require Fred to significantly downgrade his standard of living and eliminate many expenses.

Illustration A5

Fred's Age	Total Annual Income Needed	Total Annual Income Sources	Surplus/Shortage
65	$ 36,000	$ 43,020	$7,020
66	37,440	43,362	5,922
67	38,938	43,711	4,773
68	40,495	44,067	3,572
69	42,115	44,430	2,315
70	43,800	44,800	1,000
71	45,551	45,177	(374)
72	47,374	45,563	(1,811)
73	49,268	45,955	(3,313)
74	51,239	46,356	(4,883)
75	53,289	46,765	(6,524)
76	55,420	47,182	(8,239)
77	57,637	47,607	(10,030)
78	59,943	48,041	(11,902)
79	62,340	48,483	(13,857)
80	64,834	48,934	(15,900)
81	67,427	49,395	(18,033)
82	70,124	49,864	(20,260)
83	72,929	50,343	(22,586)
84	75,847	50,831	(25,015)
85	78,880	51,330	(27,551)
86	82,036	51,838	(30,198)
87	85,317	52,356	(32,961)

Illustration A5-(*Continued*)

Fred's Age	Total Annual Income Needed	Total Annual Income Sources	Surplus/Shortage
88	$88,730	$52,885	$(35,845)
89	92,279	53,424	(38,855)
90	95,970	53,974	(41,996)
91	99,809	54,535	(45,273)
92	103,801	55,108	(48,694)
93	107,953	55,692	(52,262)
94	112,271	56,287	(55,985)
95	116,762	56,894	(59,868)
96	121,433	57,514	(63,919)
97	126,290	58,146	(68,144)
98	131,342	58,790	(72,552)
99	136,595	59,448	(77,148)

The above illustration was created and provided by Financial Profiles, Inc.

Fred's example shows why it is imperative that you accumulate assets that continue to grow at a rate equal to or greater than the long term rate of after-tax inflation.

So, how do you accomplish this goal? There are several factors to consider. Risk tolerance is certainly one factor, as are taxes, interest rates, and the amount of assets you have saved.

Let's go back to our example of Fred to see how this could work. Assume that in addition to his pension and assets, Fred had accumulated $25,000 in savings and $50,000 in a 401(K) Plan. These are assets that Fred can use to offset inflation. In **Illustration A6**, we see that these additional assets growing at 5% per year will allow Fred to maintain his desired lifestyle longer than he could with his income alone. However, this example does not leave much room for error. If Fred lives past 84, he will have outlived his assets, and will be back to making due on his monthly income.

Illustration A6

Fred's Age	Total Annual Income Needed	Total Annual Income Sources	Surplus/ (Shortage)	Total Withdrawal from Capital	Total Additions to Capital	Financial Independence Capital Available
65	$36,000	$ 43,020	$7,020	($58)	$10,808	$71,300
66	37,440	43,362	5,922	(71)	10,021	80,502
67	38,938	43,711	4,773	(82)	9,190	88,809
68	40,495	44,067	3,572	(91)	8,314	96,174
69	42,115	44,430	2,315	(97)	7,389	102,548
70	43,800	44,800	1,000	(101)	6,416	107,881
71	45,551	45,177	(374)	(506)	5,766	112,120
72	47,374	45,563	(1,811)	(2,052)	6,125	115,209
73	49,268	45,955	(3,313)	(3,664)	6,495	117,092
74	51,239	46,356	(4,883)	(5,343)	6,875	117,708
75	53,289	46,765	(6,524)	(7,092)	7,266	116,997
76	55,420	47,182	(8,239)	(8,916)	7,671	114,896
77	57,637	47,607	(10,030)	(10,816)	8,091	111,338
78	59,943	48,041	(11,902)	(12,795)	8,526	106,257
79	62,340	48,483	(13,857)	(16,771)	8,629	99,303
80	64,834	48,934	(15,900)	(19,875)	7,943	89,758
81	67,427	49,395	(18,033)	(22,541)	7,008	77,332
82	70,124	49,864	(20,260)	(25,325)	5,816	61,724
83	72,929	50,343	(22,586)	(28,233)	4,341	42,611
84	75,847	50,831	(25,015)	(31,269)	2,555	19,640
85	78,880	51,330	(27,551)	(25,091)	541	(7,478)
86	82,036	51,838	(30,198)	0	0	(37,676)
87	85,317	52,356	(32,961)	0	0	(70,637)
88	88,730	52,885	(35,845)	0	0	(106,481)
89	92,279	53,424	(38,855)	0	0	(145,336)
90	95,970	53,974	(41,996)	0	0	(187,332)
91	99,809	54,535	(45,273)	0	0	(232,605)
92	103,801	55,108	(48,694)	0	0	(281,299)
93	107,953	55,692	(52,262)	0	0	(333,561)
94	112,271	56,287	(55,985)	0	0	(389,545)
95	116,762	56,894	(59,868)	0	0	(449,413)
96	121,433	57,514	(63,919)	0	0	(513,332)
97	126,290	58,146	(68,144)	0	0	(581,477)
98	131,342	58,790	(72,552)	0	0	(654,028)
99	136,595	59,448	(77,148)	0	0	(731,176)

The above illustration was created and provided by Financial Profiles, Inc.

(Note: The varying amounts shown in the "Total Withdrawal From Capital" column account are for cash withdrawals to fund shortages, as well as for taxes due on investment income using an assumed tax bracket.)

The other aspect that can go wrong in Fred's example is if he earns less than 5% on his savings. **Illustration A7** shows the same asset base, but with only a 3% rate of return. As you can see, Fred once again depletes his savings during his lifetime, finding himself without assets by age 82.

Illustration A7

Fred's Age	Total Annual Income Needed	Total Annual Income Sources	Surplus/ (Shortage)	Total Withdrawal from Capital	Total Additions to Capital	Financial Independence Capital Available
65	$36,000	$43,020	$7,020	($ 58)	$ 9,308	$ 70,100
66	37,440	43,362	5,922	(71)	8,356	77,970
67	38,938	43,711	4,773	(82)	7,346	84,801
68	40,495	44,067	3,572	(91)	6,276	90,536
69	42,115	44,430	2,315	(97)	5,141	95,112
70	43,800	44,800	1,000	(101)	3,940	98,465
71	45,551	45,177	(374)	(506)	3,044	100,526
72	47,374	45,563	(1,811)	(2,052)	3,137	101,224
73	49,268	45,955	(3,313)	(3,664)	3,218	100,486
74	51,239	46,356	(4,883)	(5,343)	3,287	98,232
75	53,289	46,765	(6,524)	(7,092)	3,342	94,381
76	55,420	47,182	(8,239)	(8,916)	3,383	88,849
77	57,637	47,607	(10,030)	(10,816)	3,410	81,547
78	59,943	48,041	(11,902)	(12,795)	3,421	72,382
79	62,340	48,483	(13,857)	(16,771)	3,237	61,115
80	64,834	48,934	(15,900)	(19,875)	2,628	47,317
81	67,427	49,395	(18,033)	(22,541)	1,880	30,789
82	70,124	49,864	(20,260)	(25,325)	994	11,324
83	72,929	50,343	(22,586)	(14,272)	118	(11,168)
84	75,847	50,831	(25,015)	0	0	(36,183)
85	78,880	51,330	(27,551)	0	0	(63,734)

Illustration A7-(*Continued*)

Fred's Age	Total Annual Income Needed	Total Annual Income Sources	Surplus/ (Shortage)	Total Withdrawal from Capital	Total Additions to Capital	Financial Independence Capital Available
86	$82,036	$51,838	$(30,198)	0	0	(93,932)
87	85,317	52,356	(32,961)	0	0	(126,893)
88	88,730	52,885	(35,845)	0	0	(162,738)
89	92,279	53,424	(38,855)	0	0	(201,592)
90	95,970	53,974	(41,996)	0	0	(243,588)
91	99,809	54,535	(45,273)	0	0	(288,861)
92	103,801	55,108	(48,694)	0	0	(337,555)
93	107,953	55,692	(52,262)	0	0	(389,817)
94	112,271	56,287	(55,985)	0	0	(445,801)
95	116,762	56,894	(59,868)	0	0	(505,669)
96	121,433	57,514	(63,919)	0	0	(569,588)
97	126,290	58,146	(68,144)	0	0	(637,733)
98	131,342	58,790	(72,552)	0	0	(710,284)
99	136,595	59,448	(77,148)	0	0	(787,432)

The above illustration was created and provided by Financial Profiles, Inc.

If we run the scenario once again, assuming a 9% rate of return, Fred's numbers improve dramatically. With this increased rate of return Fred now enjoys financial security through his 100th birthday as shown in **Illustration A8**.

Illustration A8

Fred's Age	Total Annual Income Needed	Total Annual Income Sources	Surplus/ (Shortage)	Total Withdrawal from Capital	Total Additions to Capital	Financial Independence Capital Available
65	$36,000	$43,020	$7,020	($58)	$13,808	$73,700
66	37,440	43,362	5,922	(71)	13,621	85,782
67	38,938	43,711	4,773	(82)	13,483	97,523
68	40,495	44,067	3,572	(91)	13,405	108,961
69	42,115	44,430	2,315	(97)	13,400	120,144
70	43,800	44,800	1,000	(101)	13,483	131,130
71	45,551	45,177	(374)	(506)	14,046	141,993

Illustration A8-(*Continued*)

Fred's Age	Total Annual Income Needed	Total Annual Income Sources	Surplus/ (Shortage)	Total Withdrawal from Capital	Total Additions to Capital	Financial Independence Capital Available
72	$47,374	$45,563	$(1,811)	(2,052)	$15,797	$152,819
73	49,268	45,955	(3,313)	(3,664)	17,761	163,715
74	51,239	46,356	(4,883)	(5,343)	19,966	174,805
75	53,289	46,765	(6,524)	(7,092)	22,446	186,238
76	55,420	47,182	(8,239)	(8,916)	25,238	198,189
77	57,637	47,607	(10,030)	(10,816)	28,382	210,865
78	59,943	48,041	(11,902)	(12,795)	31,928	224,506
79	62,340	48,483	(13,857)	(16,771)	35,248	238,847
80	64,834	48,934	(15,900)	(19,875)	37,439	252,899
81	67,427	49,395	(18,033)	(22,541)	39,538	266,497
82	70,124	49,864	(20,260)	(25,325)	41,556	279,481
83	72,929	50,343	(22,586)	(28,233)	43,465	291,667
84	75,847	50,831	(25,015)	(31,269)	45,235	302,840
85	78,880	51,330	(27,551)	(34,438)	46,832	312,754
86	82,036	51,838	(30,198)	(37,747)	48,214	321,128
87	85,317	52,356	(32,961)	(41,201)	49,336	327,636
88	88,730	52,885	(35,845)	(44,806)	50,145	331,907
89	92,279	53,424	(38,855)	(48,568)	50,579	333,515
90	95,970	53,974	(41,996)	(52,495)	50,569	331,974
91	99,809	54,535	(45,273)	(56,592)	50,035	326,729
92	103,801	55,108	(48,694)	(60,867)	48,887	317,145
93	107,953	55,692	(52,262)	(69,327)	47,022	302,501
94	112,271	56,287	(55,985)	(69,981)	44,321	281,973
95	116,762	56,894	(59,868)	(74,835)	40,649	254,624
96	121,433	57,514	(63,919)	(79,899)	35,855	219,389
97	126,290	58,146	(68,144)	(85,181)	29,765	175,057
98	131,342	58,790	(72,552)	(90,689)	22,180	120,249
99	136,595	59,448	(77,148)	(96,435)	12,877	53,402

The above illustration was created and provided by Financial Profiles, Inc.

Our purpose for discussing these examples is to illustrate the importance of proper planning. At this point, hopefully you can see how narrow the margin of error can be, and how small differences in rate of return can have a big impact on how long your savings will last. This is also true for small adjustments in expenditures. Perhaps Fred would be comfortable choosing higher rates of return at retirement and would be willing to take the additional risks in order to have the opportunity to earn 9%. If not, he could also consider spending a little less each month in order for his expenses to match his returns.*

*All returns are for illustrative purposes only and not indicative of any particular investment. Investment value will fluctuate with market conditions.

Regardless of which route he decides to take, it is important that he takes the time to think this through BEFORE RETIREMENT! If Fred begins his retirement with these issues properly addressed, he can then develop an appropriate investment strategy and retirement budget. If Fred waits five or ten years after he retires to tackle these issues, he may have already made too many irreversible mistakes. There is an old adage that goes "you cannot put the toothpaste back in the tube." This saying illustrates retirement planning very well. Once your savings are gone, it can be difficult to recover and maintain your lifestyle, especially if you do not have enough income to keep up with cost of living increases.

How much is enough?

No matter which of the distribution formulas someone considers, this is a question that we hear often from our clients. "How much money should I have before I retire?" Unfortunately, it's a question that does not have just one right answer. Determining how much is enough depends upon many aspects, including future inflation rates, life expectancy, investment earnings, future tax rates, and lifestyle needs. Unfortunately, you do not have much control over some of these factors. This is why any good financial plan must be dynamic in nature. In general, when devising your plan there are a few good rules of thumb to remember:

- allow for contingencies
- realistically prepare for life events
- be conservative in your assumptions.

Remember, you can recover from many mistakes in the financial world. However, if you miscalculate your future income and asset needs, this dilemma is hard to rectify once you are retired. Here are a few specific points to remember when calculating your income needs.

- **Do not assume you will be a in lower tax bracket at retirement.** You cannot control future tax rates, and our current tax code is based on income, not on age. In most cases, Social Security income is included in taxable income and that will probably not change. Pensions, withdrawals from qualified plans (like 401K plans), and traditional IRA's also are currently taxable. In addition, many tax-free investments do not outpace inflation. Therefore, do not assume that your tax bracket will be any less than it is today.

- **Do not assume that you will spend less during retirement.** While there are expenses that decrease after retirement, there are also many that will increase. You may spend more on travel and leisure when you are retired. If you develop health problems, you may require expensive medications. Many recent retirees are shocked to discover the high costs of prescription drugs, home health care, or nursing home facilities.

- **Keep in mind that there are a finite number of things that you can work with when you are designing a retirement income plan:** You can position your investments to earn more, you can choose to spend less, you can take steps to pay less in taxes or you can delay your retirement date and work longer. Those are the main variables with which you have to work. Some people do not want to spend less, so we focus on tax planning and investment management with them. Others are not comfortable with taking the risks associated with higher returns, so we focus more on lifestyle adjustments. Sometimes, there is not anything we can do to ease the tax burden, so we focus on the factors that we can control and influence.

- **Never avoid the reality of the situation.** Simplistic solutions and "magic bullet" products never solve

> complex problems. The real trick is addressing your situation in a realistic manner and managing risk at the same time, an issue that we will discuss in the next chapter. Understanding the work that needs completed in order to accomplish your goal is half the battle. Formulating an effective plan is complicated and time-consuming, but not impossible. It just requires you to focus on the correct areas and assemble a team of professionals to help you.

Many of the topics we are discussing have historical patterns that you can take into consideration. For example, we know that inflation and average returns vary and life expectancy increases throughout the decades. In the upcoming chapter on managing risk, we will discuss some of these factors more closely.

All in all, our primary objective in this chapter is to emphasize that everyone has unique circumstances, different levels of risk tolerance, and varied comfort levels as to what constitutes "conservative planning." Although these aspects differ depending on the individual, they need to be realistically addressed in all financial plans. It is important for you to communicate with your team of professionals and develop a PLAN of attack on how to deal with these changing dynamics.

Tentacle 5

Managing Risk

Tentacle 5
MANAGING RISK

In the previous chapter we addressed the risks of outliving income and assets, and how those risks can adversely affect lifestyle. Throughout the section, we stressed the fact that most retirees simply do not have sufficient assets to allocate all of their money towards lower-return, fixed investments and live at the mercy of interest rates and inflation.>>> We begin this chapter with the same statement that ended the last chapter: **"ANY GOOD RETIREMENT PLAN MUST OUTPACE INFLATION!"** The trick, as we all know, is that this task is often easier said than done.

The raging bull market of the mid to late 1990s lulled many investors to sleep, causing many to abandon risk management and opt for the sexy sport of chasing 20 and 30 percent returns. Unfortunately, the biting bears of the early 2000s violently interrupted that dreamy slumber. Investors were again reminded that risk management should and must play a major role in investment planning.

Interestingly enough, the bear market of the early 2000s also gave birth to some creative changes in the investment world. As many investors saw their retirement savings cut in half, some lost faith in the markets. Consequently, investment companies felt their belts tighten as investors pulled their money out to sit on the sidelines. In order to stay competitive and to stay in business, many mutual fund, variable annuity, and fixed annuity companies started to create new product features designed to provide some downside protection against risk. Many of these new features appealed to investors, even though they may not have fully understood what they were purchasing. As a result of this commercial packaging of risk management, we are now faced with two distinct strategies to minimize and manage risk in retirement portfolios:

- **Utilize insurance company guarantees to minimize risk.**
- **Utilize traditional methods of asset allocation.**

The first of the methods…utilizing insurance or mutual fund guarantees, involves a very wide array of product choices, features, costs, and benefits. Please understand that each one of these topics could have volumes of technical explanation printed about it. It would be impossible to effectively cover all of these methods and tools within the scope of this book, and the industry of "packaged products" is so dynamic that product information becomes quickly outdated and obsolete.

There are however, a few things that can be said about the guarantees offered by mutual fund and annuity companies that will always be applicable. The golden rule of these inherent truths is that no company provides any guarantee for free. In other words…you will pay somehow, some way for any guarantee that is offered. This cost may come in the form of a flat fee, an annual charge, a limit or cap of investment return, or through extended surrender penalties, but it will exist in some form. Because of this it is extremely important to research any financial product offering minimum guarantees. When doing this research, there is a good rule of thumb where to begin:

Security or Non-security?

Products that are registered as "securities" have very strict and stringent rules that govern the disclosure of fees and risks, and must be sold under a prospectus, which is an official disclosure that must be provided to an investor prior to or at the point of sale. Reading the prospectus thoroughly is very important because this is where all costs and legal definitions will be clearly outlined. Any time a relevant change is made within a registered security, the prospectus must be updated to reflect and disclose those changes.

Financial products that are not registered as securities are not subject to the prospectus rule. Oftentimes, these products fall under the jurisdiction of state insurance regulations which are generally much less stringent and carry different disclosure requirements. Furthermore, individuals who sell these products need not be registered with any federal or state securities commission, and therefore do not have the same level of supervision or compliance requirements as securities licensed individuals.

Because of the technical and dynamic nature of packaged product guarantees, we cannot stress enough the importance of researching the details inherent in each product. This only strengthens our earlier recommendations about working with a team of financial professionals. We suggest you refer to the upcoming chapter "Putting Together the Right Team" before considering any purchase of financial products or investments.

Before the recent boom of financial product guarantees and protection riders, there was a more traditional and time tested method of reducing risk. In fact, you probably learned it long ago with the old adage "Don't put all your eggs in one basket". Not putting all of your eggs in one basket makes sense, and the same can be said with your investments. Diversification of investments is a simple concept, but this simple concept has become the genesis of thousands of studies and decades of research. Over the years this research has developed into the science of asset allocation.

Asset allocation is the process of using different asset classes, primarily cash, bonds, stocks, and real estate in order to customize risk exposure within a portfolio. By controlling how much money is invested in each asset class, we can influence the amount of volatility to which an investment portfolio is exposed. In turn, this creates results that form historical patterns. As we study these trends, we understand how percentage combinations create different results over time, which could be described as the basis for the science of asset allocation. Some of these trends can be surprising. For instance, most people instinctively assume that a portfolio consisting of cash and bonds would provide the ultimate "safe" portfolio. Decades of research however, show that the addition of a broad stock index into the portfolio can actually reduce risk and volatility over time. Diversifying the duration of the bonds and the type of stocks within a portfolio can reduce risk further. The addition of real estate, the percentage of asset classes, and the diversification of industry and business sectors, are all factors that can be modified to produce very different risk and reward profiles. Much like changing the ingredients in a recipe, these factors can be changed to create an optimum investment portfolio which matches a client's needs, goals and tolerance for risk. Skillful management of this process can be extremely effective in the mitigation of risk.

How effective can asset allocation be? During the past two decades, there have been many professional studies conducted concerning the importance of asset allocation. The vast majority of these studies all indicate that asset allocation plays an important role in the success or failure of a portfolio. Gary P. Brinson, Randolph L. Hood, and Gilbert L. Beebower conducted one of the most well-known studies entitled, "Determinants of Portfolio Performance." This study was published in the *Financial Analysts Journal* in January/February 1995, and was a follow up from their original study done in 1986. This study is well-known within the financial services industry because it concluded that asset allocation accounted for more than 90% of the difference in the investment return of portfolios. This conclusion was profound because it suggested that the factors most investors spent the majority of their time researching were almost inconsequential. Factors such as individual investment selection, market timing and costs have traditionally been where most investors focus their attention. However, this study concluded that those factors made up less than 10% of a client's success or failure – and that it is asset allocation that affects a portfolio's success most of all.

One of the criticisms of the Brinson study is that it conducted its analysis using 91 large corporate pension plans with assets more than $100 million dollars. While this was excellent data for the purposes of analyzing pension assets, many financial analysts believe that it may not be appropriate for drawing conclusions about the average retiree's investment portfolio. Individual investors are affected by other factors such as cash flow dynamics, individual taxes, different expense structures, and many more. We feel that the truth rests somewhere in the middle. Factors such as expenses, taxes, and cash flow affect individual investors more than they affect large pension plans. At the same time, the powerful findings of asset allocation studies should not be ignored.

The breadth of information and research available on the subject of asset allocation is enormous. It is our feeling that trying to duplicate that research here is unnecessary. Instead, we would like to suggest a few sources of information that we believe will give you a strong foundational understanding of the importance and power of asset allocation.

Some of the most important and influential work on asset allocation was conducted by Harry M. Markowitz. Mr. Markowitz developed the economic theory known as Modern Portfolio Theory. His work was first published under the title "Portfolio Selection" in the 1952 Journal of Finance. This is an excellent source for understanding the science which supports asset allocation.

Another excellent source for information is Ibbotson Associates, a leading authority on asset allocation founded by Professor Roger Ibbotson in 1977. The company is a well-respected resource for professional advisors and has spent over 25 years providing research and development in the areas of asset allocation, investment management services, and educational materials. More information about Ibbotson can be found at www.ibbotson.com.

Now that we have illustrated the importance of asset allocation, we want to caution you. Proper asset allocation involves more than entering your age into a software program and receiving a computer-generated list of stock, bond, and cash percentages. Many mutual fund companies now offer interactive asset allocation tools on their web sites. These tools allow investors to enter a few bits of information and receive a generic model portfolio to follow. We do not believe that this represents thorough asset allocation planning. Many dynamic factors are involved in the proper construction of a portfolio. No "cookie cutter" approach could possibly address these variables correctly. Understanding asset allocation is like peeling back the layers of an onion. Each layer reveals new complexities and innovative concepts to understand. For instance, all stocks are not the same. Large cap stocks do not behave the same as small cap stocks. Short-term bonds do not behave like long-term bonds. Growth stocks differ from value stocks, and there are many factors that contribute to define a bond's risk. Let's not forget that stocks or bonds in the United States do not necessarily operate the way they do in Europe, Asia, or other parts of the world. In addition to stocks, bonds, and cash positions, real estate can be used to create some interesting effects in a portfolio's risk and return. Therefore, asset allocation is in fact a science, and perhaps even an art.

Furthermore, asset allocation is an ongoing and dynamic

process which is why active portfolio management plays such a crucial role. Portfolios need to change according to market dynamics, client needs, tax laws, expenses, changes specific to the investments themselves and an ever changing landscape of circumstantial variables. Given the importance and the complexity of the process, it is an area that you should pay special attention to in your retirement planning In our opinion, we believe that knowledge of asset allocation and portfolio management should be among your top priorities when developing your financial plan, and putting together your financial team.

We have examined how the mutual fund and annuity industries are providing solutions to manage risk. We also discussed how the science of asset allocation and active portfolio management can be an accurate compass for risk management. Keep in mind that by combining these strategies, you can create unlimited planning models to complement your individual needs and wants.

This once again highlights the importance of a theme that you are seeing throughout this book:

** **PUT THE PLANNING BEFORE THE PRODUCTS** **

In our experience, if there is one single mistake that we consistently see people making in retirement planning, is that they have sporadically purchased products and investments based on highlights, features, or sizzle. These individuals most often did so without ever stepping back to analyze and understand how those products would fit into their overall risk tolerance, tax scenario, and distribution plan. To buy a product or invest compulsively without properly planning is the ultimate risk. At this point, we hope you will take the concepts presented in this chapter and use them in conjunction with the other critical parts of retirement planning. Remember, there are eight tentacles to the retirement octopus, and they all need to work together!

Tentacle 6

Protecting Your Family

Tentacle 6
Protecting Your Family

Nothing seems to cause a person's eyes to glaze over faster than a conversation about insurance. I think we all understand that insurance is an inherently important aspect of planning for our family's financial security, but the questions of how much, and what kind to purchase are always a topic of great debate.

Let's talk life insurance...

There is an old saying – if you ask a life insurance agent how much life insurance you should own, they'll always tell you that you should own some more. The unfortunate thing is... this is all too often the truth. People often make the decision to purchase some kind of life insurance coverage early in their family life, and never really update it as their financial situation changes.

Although the question of how much you need is a personal decision, there are some good guidelines and concepts which can be used to determine an approximate range of coverage which may be appropriate for your own situation. One method which is often found in the popular press (which many times is merely shameless self-promotion and misinformation), is a system comprised of a simple multiplier of income, generally 10 times income. This approach is ludicrously simplistic and devoid of any intelligent thought. Only amateurs and product hawkers resort to this approach. So how does an intelligent person determine an appropriate amount?

First and foremost, the question which must be answered, is, "How much life insurance do you want to own, so as to ensure your family's lifestyle is maintained at a level they are accustomed to?" That may sound like an easy question, but the answer is always very different for different people. The purchase of life insurance is really an expression of love and concern for the well-being of your family. If life insurance were free, I'm sure most of us would own as much as they would give us. But as we all know, it isn't free, so the economics of the decision as to how much we really want greatly affects the amount we have. Hence, we often choose to own an amount which doesn't necessarily match what we need. Maintaining a standard of living can mean completely different things to different families. There is no right or wrong answer as to how much insurance is needed to maintain the family's lifestyle. There exists an entire wide range of family needs that need to be protected. Some people have enough other financial assets, and therefore need no life insurance. Unfortunately, most of us aren't that fortunate.

This leads to the discussion of what we believe is the proper way to determine an appropriate amount of coverage. We assume of course, that the proposed insured person wishes to provide for his or her family. The core concept for determining a realistic amount of insurance is called the human life value. Unfortunately though, this concept can be interpreted several different ways.

This concept is often used by the U.S. Courts system in determining awards for wrongful death claims. In the basic application, the amount which is awarded (minus pain and suffering) is the projected future earnings of the decedent. If a man or woman age 45, earning $50,000 per year is wrongfully killed, then the amount of the award would be $50,000 times 20 (the number of years until retirement), or one million dollars. Several other factors should also be considered, including lost retirement savings, costs of replacement for non-employment activities, etc., etc.

Although such an approach is clearly better than the aforementioned multiplier of earnings approach, it is still too simplistic an approach for your authors. Factors such as future increases in earnings, cost of living, and various other outside factors such as accumulated and lost retirement benefits, medical benefits, education savings, and emotional consequences all should be included in the calculations. Any good financial planner worth his\her own salt should be able to assist in calculating all these factors, and help you arrive at a lump-sum amount which would satisfy your goals and desires.

Over the course of our careers, we've heard all the arguments made for every different type of life insurance, and why each and every type is better than all the others. At the risk of sounding as if we prefer one type of life insurance over the others, our opinion as to the proper kind of insurance to buy is as follows:

The two most important factors driving the decision process should be 1) affordability, and 2) the timeframe over which the coverage is required. All too often, the time in life when people need the largest amount of coverage, is when they have the least amount of discretionary income, i.e. when they are young and have families to protect. The most logical solution to this problem is the longer (20-30 year) level term products, which are widely available. As the need for larger amounts of coverage reduces – as savings accumulate, children educated, etc., - then the need for the large initial coverage diminishes, and may even ultimately cease. However, please do not construe this to mean that we are recommending term insurance over other forms of cash value insurance. We are actually advocates of a combination approach. By this, I mean that we believe the best way to protect all your life insurance needs is to cover those larger short-term risks with the term insurance, and longer-term\permanent needs with cash value insurance. By longer-term, we mean the desire to protect your loved ones long after the children have left the nest, and you're planning for your retirement years.

The reason we advocate this approach, comes back to the issue of affordability. If you purchase the long-term cash value insurance when you are young, you are using the power of long-term compounding to provide an affordable solution for when you are older. Please note that we have been very careful not to say that cash value insurance guarantees a smaller or fixed premium, as only whole life and its derivatives guarantee a fixed premium for life. It is the excess premiums paid, over and above the death benefit costs and administrative expenses, which are paid into a cash value product that accumulates and provides a cushion against the ever increasing death benefit costs as you age.

You may be wondering which type of cash value life insurance is the best to own, or appropriate to suit your needs. The answer to this question depends upon your feelings about investment risk. As in any investment, the greater the risk you assume, the greater the potential for return or loss. Accordingly, the more risk the insurance company assumes, with respect to future cash values, the smaller the potential return or risk of loss.

The point is, most people have a desire to own life insurance coverage, well beyond the point in life where there will be a major detrimental economic impact on their loved ones lifestyles should they die. Whether for inheritance purposes, or to simplify a surviving spouse's economic life, the best time to purchase cash value insurance is when you are young. The cost of purchasing cash value insurance when you are older is often cost prohibitive. For this reason, we reiterate our strong advocacy of purchasing both kinds of insurance when you are younger. Of course, every individual's circumstances will differ, and our general approach as outlined above may not fit your own situation.

The best way to approach the process of purchasing life insurance is the same as any other major purchase you make in life. Take the time to educate yourself with respect to your options, and seek the advice of a professional. We realize this may not be an easy task, especially when an insurance agent is not working for you, but rather for the company. Request a proposal from several (at least three) professionals. You will be amazed at the variety of solutions you will be confronted with. As a last step, I would even consider paying a good, knowledgeable, and independent financial planner to evaluate the various proposals you've received. The extra money and time you invest in this major financial decision will be well spent.

II) Disability Insurance

Disability insurance is probably one of the least understood types of insurance coverage. Even most dedicated insurance agents often have only a cursory understanding of the various intricacies of disability insurance.

When we prepare a retirement analysis/plan for a working couple, we often have to make a determined effort to uncover the true nature of the extent to which they are protected by disability insurance. All too often, when asked about their disability coverage, the answer we get is "we're covered at work." When pressed as to what that means, the most common response is a shrug of the shoulders.

Now, you might be wondering why a discussion about disability insurance is an important part of retirement planning. When we devise a retirement plan, one of the major assumptions that we make, is that you will maintain meaningful employment until you attain your targeted retirement age. However, if you were to become disabled, you will most likely not be capable of maintaining that same level of employment. Not only are you not working, earning the same level of income to support your lifestyle, but you are also not accruing retirement benefits, and probably incurring extra medical costs. It's a triple whammy to your retirement plan! According to recent statistics, you are far more likely to incur a disability prior to retirement than you are likely to die.

We've addressed the planning for the possibility of death, and how that can easily be incorporated as a contingency within a retirement plan. Planning for a disability is no different, but represents it's own unique set of challenges.

Death is an easily definable event. The diagnosis of a disability is not as cut and dried. Insurance companies, employers, and consumers seldom agree as to when a malady represents a situation which precludes working. Not only is it hard to define when it is that you might be incapable of working, but it is often even harder to determine when it is that you are capable of returning to work.

As a consequence of this dilemma, insurance companies have drafted very precise and complicated legal contracts regarding disability insurance. It is extremely important to work with an insurance agent or planner that specializes in disability coverage. This is especially true if you want to evaluate an existing policy, or are considering the purchase of new/additional coverage. If you are one of those people who are "covered at work," we highly recommend you do some serious homework, and really find out all you can about that coverage. Go out and get two or three opinions regarding the terms and value of that coverage. Unfortunately, it is our experience that most employer-sponsored group plans are extremely lacking with respect to the perceived benefits. We find, that most people believe they don't need to be concerned about their disability coverage, when in reality they really should be.

The details concerning what constitutes good, or even appropriate coverage is well beyond the scope of this text. The types, terms, and conditions under which policies are issued far outnumber the options and variations of life insurance policies.

As a final thought, we'd like to re-emphasize our position on the importance of good disability insurance coverage. There is an old fable used by the disability insurance agents, which is a great story. It's the fable of the goose that laid the golden eggs. Today, far too many people worry about insuring the golden eggs. We insure our homes, cars, and other worldly possessions. But doesn't it make more sense to insure the goose that lays the eggs? It is our ability to continue to work and earn an income that allows us to buy and maintain the home, car, boat, and all the other things we have. Without our income, where would most of us find ourselves? If we were to become disabled, without an income, life could very well become a living nightmare. Without a doubt, this area of planning is often overlooked, but really deserves serious consideration.

Tentacle

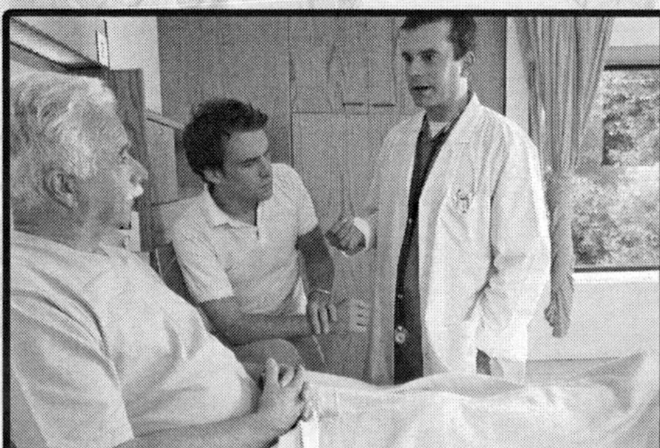

Preventing Medical & Long-Term Care Costs from Consuming Your Retirement Assets

Tentacle 7

Preventing Medical & Long-Term Care Costs from Consuming Your Retirement Assets

The subject of long-term care expenses is a topic that few like to discuss. However, if this issue is not properly addressed, long-term care related expenses can derail the best retirement plan. Throughout this publication, we have stressed that each arm of the retirement octopus is complex, and a complete and thorough exploration of each is beyond the scope of this book. Our intent has been to cover each subject in a manner that highlights the priorities and provides direction to properly address each issue. This statement is especially true in this chapter for a number of reasons. First, the subject of long-term care is enormous in its breadth, and we could not cover everything in one book, let alone a single chapter. Second, long-term care factors are very dynamic in nature, and are changing everyday. Therefore, we will once again focus on the fundamental areas to assist you in your planning process.

For most workers, the majority of medically related expenses are handled by their group or individual health insurance. That scenario normally changes as individuals become eligible for Medicare. As we covered in our Medicare/Medicaid chapter, most retirees stop relying on private major medical coverage at that time. Instead, they will most likely rely on a combination of Medicare and Medicare supplemental insurances (Medigap). The key issue to understand is that this combination of coverage can be tailored to cover almost any **medical** expenses you will experience during your senior years. But, none of these sources of coverage will pay for **long-term care** expenses. As a result, planning for these costs needs to be addressed in a separate section of your retirement plan.

What is long-term care? – When most people hear the phrase "long-term care," they often think a nursing home. While some seniors do require 24-hour nursing home care during their later years, that arrangement does not necessarily represent the majority of long-term care scenarios. Studies show that a greater number of individuals will receive long-term care in the form of home health care or assisted living. Current statistics can be found at www.aarp.com.

Home Health Care – Home health care can include a very broad list of services that are normally administered outside of an institutional setting. These may include: part-time skilled nursing care, physical and/or occupational therapy, part-time services from home health aides, help from homemakers, the purchase or rental of medical equipment and emergency alert systems, modifications to the home such as ramps for a wheelchair or bathroom modifications, adult day care, respite care, caregiver training of family members or friends, prescription drugs, and laboratory services typically provided in hospitals and nursing homes.

Assisted Living – Assisted living is for those individuals who may no longer be able to completely care for themselves, yet they do not need as high a level of skilled care that is provided in a nursing home. We think this is a good time to discuss **Continuing Care Retirement Communities (CCRC's)**, which are growing in popularity and numbers in recent years. Residents in a CCRC facility pay an entrance fee that allows them to move into an apartment, condominium, or townhouse. Normally, a monthly fee is paid that includes meals, housecleaning, and varying degrees of healthcare. If a resident's health declines and they are in need of higher levels of care, they can move to the assisted living or nursing home portion of the CCRC.

Who does and does not pay for long term care expenses? Many individuals believe that Medicare or Medicaid will pay for long-term care – this is a common misconception. Here are some basic facts regarding how Medicare and Medicaid treat long-term care expenses.

Medicare's skilled nursing facility (SNF) benefit DOES NOT cover the cost of most nursing home care. Medicare normally pays only if…

- the beneficiary has first received inpatient hospital care for at least three nights, and entered a skilled nursing facility within 30 days of that hospital stay.
- the beneficiary entered the skilled nursing facility for

the same medical reason that required the hospital stay.

- there is an expectation of recovery. (Medicare usually will NOT pay for chronic conditions.)

Even if the above conditions are met, Medicare still does not cover:

- Homemaker services
- Personal care unless you are homebound and also receiving skilled care and expected to recover.

The important thing to remember about Medicare is that it is designed to provide medical care, not long-term or custodial care. Under certain circumstances, Medicare supplement insurance may pay a small amount towards long term care expenses. However, this does little to ease the financial burden, considering average long-term care costs.

Medicaid will pay for care in a skilled nursing facility if your monthly income is less than $1,693, based on 2004 figures. In addition, your assets must be between $18,552.00 and $92,760.00* (depending on marital status, etc.). It will not pay for custodial care unless skilled care is also required.

As you can see, Medicare and Medicaid are not the solutions to long-term care costs for anyone with moderate income or assets.

So how do you pay for long-term care? – Currently, there are only three ways to pay for long-term care expenses.

- Self-insure
- Purchase traditional long-term care insurance, or
- Utilize newer multi-benefit insurance products that have long-term care components.

Before we examine each of these options, we first need to discuss the cost of long-term care, a very important reality.

The following numbers are from AARP study entitled "Beyond 50: A Report to the Nation on Independent Living and Disability, 2003". (www.research.aarp.org)

- Average national cost for nursing home stay- $55,000 per year
- Average cost for home health care worker - $18 per hour
- Estimates of Average Assisted Living expenses - $21,600 to $26,300 per year

When you consider a 5% annual compounded rate of inflation on these costs, you see that the average expense for skilled nursing facilities could exceed $100,000 per year as early as 2015.

As you can see, it is vitally important to consider long-term care expenses when designing your financial plan. Self-insuring, the first option we listed, is not affordable for most people. If one spouse needs long-term care, the other spouse still needs a place to live. In other words, the couple is still responsible for the same standard living expenses in addition to the long-term care costs. Furthermore, the estimates we quoted above only cover the cost of services that are provided in a facility. They do not include other basic expenses such as personal care, entertainment, meals outside of a facility, and other normal living expenses. Most retirement plans could not support an additional $55,000 per year on top of normal retirement needs. Even when a person's or couple's income and assets are large enough to cover these costs, it would require sacrificing in other areas.

Other options – The other way to accommodate for long-term care is to purchase some type of additional insurance coverage. While many types of policies within the insurance industry are relatively standardized, such as life, auto, and homeowners insurance, this is not true with long-term care insurance. In the long-term care industry, there are significant differences between the policies issued by different companies. You will find that benefits and features will vary greatly from one insurance company to another. The differing factors include the types of care covered, how benefits are paid, how long they are paid, how benefits are triggered, and whether insurance premiums are tax deductible. While there are many variances among long-term care policies, there are standard categories of benefits that will usually be addressed. We will review some of these aspects to help you make educated policy comparisons.

What types of care are covered? – Within the long-term care industry, there are policies which cover only facility-based care or only home health care. There are also comprehensive care policies which combine both of these benefits. A good comprehensive policy should provide benefits for nursing home, custodial, assisted living, hospice, Alzheimer's, home health, and adult day care.

How are benefits paid in long-term care policies? –Most long-term care policies are structured to pay daily benefits. When purchasing a policy, you will be asked to select the amount of the daily benefit, generally in increments of $10 per day. Benefits are typically designed by the insurance agent to coincide with the average room rate for nursing home facilities in their geographic areas. Most insurance companies will set limits on this amount. Generally, daily benefits do not exceed $200-$250, which in most instances would suffice. In addition to selecting a dollar amount, you will also choose how long you want the benefit to be paid. Common benefit periods range from as little as one year to as long as a lifetime. Keep in mind that most policies also have an elimination period, which is the length of time that must pass after long-term care commences but before benefit payments begin (similar to a deductible). Time periods for these deductibles may be as low as 0 days, or as long as 365 days.

Another variance that affects how benefits are paid is

whether the policy pays on a reimbursement or a per diem basis. Reimbursement contracts refund the insured for actual expenses incurred up to the maximum limit. For example, if a person's daily limit is $200, but the actual expense incurred is only $140, the policy will only pay $140. On the other hand, per diem policies pay the actual benefit amount of the policy regardless of the actual expense. So, in the same example, a per diem policy would pay the full $200 even if the actual cost was only $140. Some insurers also offer a version of the per diem policy which will pay benefits once the insured satisfies the benefit triggers of the contract, regardless if long term care is being provided. These are referred to as disability-based policies.

When are benefits paid? – In the previous paragraph, we used the term ***"benefit triggers."*** This term refers to the set of circumstances that must occur in order for you to qualify for benefits and when your elimination period begins, if applicable. Almost all policies will use ***Activities of Daily Living (ADL's)*** in order to determine benefit triggers. These ADL's were defined by the Health Insurance Portability and Accountability Act of 1996 (HIPPAA). This act defines six activities of daily living which include eating, bathing, dressing, transferring from bed to chair, using the toilet, and maintaining continence. Most policies will state that a person has to be unable to fulfill two of the six ADL's in order to qualify for benefits. Again, since policies and insurance companies vary drastically, some may require two of five ADL's. This is one area that can differ greatly among long-term care policies. Therefore, potential buyers should pay close attention when comparing plans. Cognitive impairment (diminished mental capacity) is also a benefit trigger in most policies, even if one is able to perform all of the ADL's.

Another common variance between insurance companies that will affect benefits is how the elimination period is calculated. Some policies will count only those days that actual services were provided. Others will count a calendar week as seven days if there were any services at all provided during that week. (For instance, if a patient received three actual days of home health service, this would still be counted as a full seven day week.) These two methods can result in drastically different time periods depending upon circumstances. For example, let's say an individual has a 90-day elimination period and receives home health services four days per week. In the first method, it would take 22 weeks to satisfy the 90-day elimination period, while the second calculation method would begin to pay after 13 weeks.

It is important to remember that there can be a great amount of variance between different insurance companies and their insurance contracts. Below is a list of questions to research when considering a long-term care policy:

- How are the premiums paid?
- Are the premium amounts guaranteed?
- Is the policy guaranteed renewable?

- Are there any features for inflation protection?
- Is there a spousal discount available?
- Is the policy tax qualified or non-tax qualified?
- What are the policies non-forfeiture options?
- Does the policy allow for restoration of benefits?
- What is the financial rating of the insurance company?

Obviously some of these questions are technical in nature. Before purchasing long-term care insurance, we recommend that you work with a licensed professional who can explain how these questions apply to your specific situation, and to the specific insurance plan you are considering.

When we start to contemplate the unpleasant realities of long-term care, there is a natural tendency to procrastinate. As we conclude this chapter, we want to mention two common objections some folks may raise when considering this type of addition to their financial plan, and provide some cautionary facts to help you approach the topic of long-term care.

It isn't going to happen to me! – This is probably the most common reaction people have when confronting long-term care. The facts confirm you may not need these types of services. Statistics from the Department of Health and Human Services indicate that people who are 65 or older face a 40 percent chance of entering a nursing home. Therefore, 60 percent will not enter a nursing home! However, remember that not all long-term care related expenses involve a nursing home. You may receive care at home before utilizing any type of facility, if at all.

Also, keep in mind that continuing advances in medical science have increased human life expectancy – we are living longer than ever. In the past, most people that required long-term care were likely to have suffered a stroke or other acute disease. Because of longer life spans, a majority of the elderly population become incapacitated by chronic conditions such as arthritis, osteoporosis, heart and lung disease, and Alzheimer's. Many with these types of conditions require assistance with daily functions, and the likelihood of needing some form of long-term care is increased.

As with all risk planning, you need to weigh the possibility of needing protection against the ability to survive without coverage. If your financial plan shows large weaknesses in its ability to fund long-term care expenses on your own, you cannot afford to ignore it as a planning priority.

My kids/family will take care of me. – While this sounds like an easy and comforting solution, it is not often realistic. More often than not, family members are simply not capable of providing the level of care that their elders require. Other factors such as geographic dispersion of family members, increased participation in the workforce by women and children, and higher divorce rates make this option less and less viable. Even in situations where family members can provide the care, this almost always causes financial strain and hardship on the caregivers, impacting their own savings and retirement goals.

When is long-term care insurance appropriate? – There are a great number of factors to consider when deciding whether or not you should purchase long-term care insurance. You should probably NOT buy long-term care insurance if you have limited assets, your only source of income is Social Security or Supplemental Social Security Income (SSI), you are on Medicaid, or you cannot afford the premiums.

You should consider buying long-term care insurance if you have significant assets and income which you want to protect, you can pay the premiums without financial difficulty, and if independence and flexibility in choosing the type and location of care is important to you.

As with all of the topics discussed in this book, it is our strong opinion that you should thoroughly analyze your financial situation before you shop around for long-term care insurance policies. Put the plan before the product, and then let your financial plan indicate whether you need to purchase additional insurance. This philosophy also raises an important final point. If you do purchase long-term care insurance, make sure you structure the policy to cover your needs instead of only worrying about the cost. In other words, just because nursing homes in your area cost $140 per day does not necessarily mean that you need to purchase that exact amount of coverage. Most people have income and assets that can be used towards long-term care costs. As we said previously, the majority of retirees do not have enough income and assets to cover extreme examples of long-term care scenarios. However, at the same time, most people have some income and assets that can be applied. For this reason, you may not need to insure 100 percent of the cost. This is just one more example of why addressing all eight arms of the retirement plan is so important. Put the plan before the product!

Tentacle 8

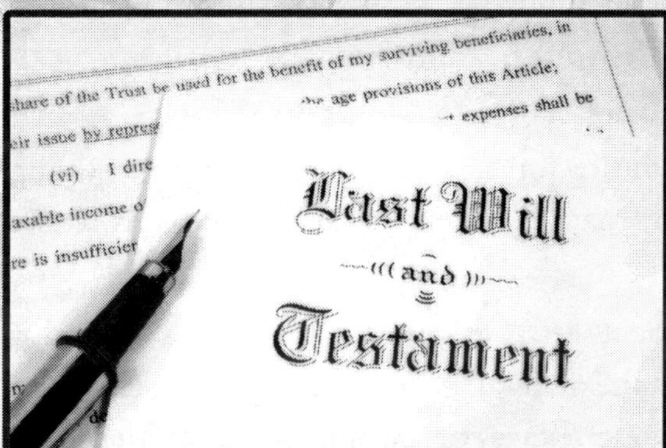

Basic Estate Planning

Tentacle 8
Basic Estate Planning

Estate planning seems to be the one tentacle of the retirement planning octopus that concerns almost every client we see, but is also the one area that few of them want to address. Perhaps many people are so busy in their lives that they do not give it due consideration. But we believe the real reason is that most people view death as the logical successor to retirement, hence, the reluctance to give it serious thought. We tend to think that, what we don't contemplate won't possibly happen.

Most people consider estate planning to be an extremely complex and technical topic. The good news, though, is that for the vast majority of Americans, it only involves some basic planning.

The federal estate tax is in a transitional period right now. Currently the federal government gives each of us a credit against the estate taxes that would be owed. The credit basically protects $1.5 million of an individual's assets from taxation, or $3 million per couple (with proper planning). That exemption increases to $3.5 million in 2009, and under current tax law the estate tax itself is fully repealed in 2010. This law will expire due to the infamous sunset provisions. These provisions provide for certain laws to expire automatically at the end of a specified period of time unless renewed by new legislation. In this case, the tax magically reappears in 2011, back at the 2001 tax exemption rate of $1 million per person. Congress is currently attempting to rectify this situation through changes in the law, and we believe that it will develop the backbone required to bring about a permanent change to the federal tax rules in this area.

So, how do you plan today for such a transitory tax? As we stated above, the vast majority of Americans have not accumulated more than $2 million of assets, so it is only the basics of which they need be concerned. Even those with estates which exceed $2 million should really tend to the basics before they get involved in some of the more exotic tools of the estate planning trade. It is our sincere belief that although there has been a lot of talk about a full repeal of the estate tax system, ultimately Congress will come to some form of compromise. We believe this will probably be a permanent increase in the exemption amount. A larger exemption would allow small business owners and farmers, whose families have been hit the hardest by this tax, to pass assets to their children without incurring significant federal taxes.

So, what are the basics of estate planning? Knowledge and action are two basic components of estate planning. Over the years, we have met many professional seminar attendees who have an excellent grasp of the basics. However, they are still searching for that magic bullet solution to all their concerns and they still have not taken any actions to plan their estate. All you need to know are some of the fundamental rules and apply them. Without taking action, knowledge will never solve their problems.

Where do you begin? Well, first understand that any and all

assets pass to your heirs in one of only four ways:

1) Beneficiary Designation

2) Legal Contract

3) Will

4) Trust

You can now begin to review your assets and documents with respect to the above list. Start with your beneficiary designations and proceed down the list.

Step 1) Review all your assets that have beneficiary designations including life insurance, IRAs, qualified plans, and group benefits. Ensure that those designations are current and updated. We encounter many clients that discover their group life insurance beneficiary designations have never updated to reflect changes. It is always fun to show a husband or wife that the ex-spouse is still the beneficiary of their benefits. Suddenly, action comes to the forefront! Another mistake we see is having minors designated as the beneficiary. Since minors by definition cannot legally obligate themselves (sign documents) – the plan/insurance company cannot pay the benefit directly to the minor. The plan/company needs a legal release of their obligation (signature). The end result is often a long and possibly costly delay in getting benefits to those minors. Therefore, avoid naming minors as beneficiaries.

Assets which are transferred via beneficiary designations avoid probate. Probate is the actual process in which a court oversees the distribution of property left by your will, and ensures that your directives are carried out. We will be discussing probate later, but generally there is a cost to probate an asset. For this reason, any process which bypasses probate, such as beneficiary designations, is a good idea. There is an exception to this rule. It is possible to name your own estate as the beneficiary of these types of assets. This action would then subject those assets to probate. Generally, this is a bad idea, although there are some advanced planning techniques in which it may be beneficial. Unless you have received good legal counsel to name your estate as a beneficiary, we would suggest you avoid doing so.

The best part of transferring assets via beneficiary designation is that it is absolutely free. It is such an important part of a good estate plan and there is no cost to implement this step. The time you spend working on these details is time well spent.

Step 2) Review all legal documents to which you are a party. The most common documents that we come across are property deeds and business ownership documents. There are several different ways to own property. Each form affects the tax ramifications and ownership of that property after death. The other complicating factor is the state laws regarding ownership rights. The nuances of the various forms of ownership are beyond the scope of this discussion. The main point to remember is that if you own any asset via a legal contract; understand the results of the dissolution of that contract upon your death. The most common example of this is determining home ownership upon your passing. This may seem simple, but what happens when you have complicated circumstances such as a second marriage or a longtime family homestead? Review your state ownership rules and take action to ensure the property will be transferred as you wish.

Step 3) Write a will. This is oftentimes the most important process. If an asset has not been transferred via a beneficiary designation or a legal contract, it will be transferred via your will. Your will is really the foundation of your estate plan. Its importance can not be overstated. It is the means by which your intentions are carried out and your assets are transferred.

There are numerous potential pitfalls in the design of a will. However, the biggest mistake is not having a will at all. If you die without a will, otherwise known as intestacy, the state in which you reside has a canned will for you. Surprisingly, in most states, a surviving spouse does not receive all the assets. Because of these types of stipulations, you will probably not like the terms of the state's will. After the inevitable occurs, it will be too late to draft a will. Ensure you have a proper will!

Another common problem we see is clients that have wills with extremely outdated information. Often we see wills that were created 20 or 30 years ago. As you may know, life can change in the matter of a day. Almost everyone's life has changed during the past few decades. Remember that your will has to stay abreast of these changes.

When writing a will, there are three key participants that are always involved in this process. The person for whom the will exists is also known as the draftee/testator. The executor\

executrix is the person you have named to be responsible for ensuring that your will is executed in the manner that you have dictated in the document. The beneficiaries are the individuals that receive the assets. Keeping your will current also involves reviewing these key people to make sure that they still meet the criteria to be in their respective roles. Is he/she still alive? Can he/she be found? Is he/she reliable? Does he/she want this responsibility? People and circumstances change over time and your will should reflect these changes.

There are four areas we frequently encounter which often require clients to draft new wills. There are more scenarios, but these are the most common:

1) Re-marriage
2) Moving to a different state
3) Old automatic clauses
4) Specific dollar bequests

The need for changing your will following a re-marriage is pretty self-explanatory. When children are involved, the issues become exponentially complicated. Therefore, we recommend professional assistance in these cases. While moving to another state may not seem to be a reason to review your will, keep in mind that every state has its own set of rules and regulations regarding estates and wills. Ensure your will is valid within the state in which it will be probated.

Automatic clauses are generally a good idea, but require constant monitoring. An example of an automatic clause in a will is one that would automatically take assets from the first spouse that dies and place them in a trust, rather than being left directly to the surviving spouse. The amount of those assets automatically adjusts to the exemption amount we discussed previously. We have seen old wills which were drafted prior to the current law, and have remained unchanged even though there have been approximately 15 to 20 significant changes to the estate tax laws in the last 35 years. Certain automatic clauses in some of these wills could leave the surviving spouse essentially penniless. Pay close attention to these types of clauses and make sure you or your adviser stay abreast of any law changes.

Specific bequests can also be a dangerous clause if you do not monitor them as your situation changes. For example, many people designate a charity or distant relative to be a beneficiary of a specific bequest. Let's say you name XYZ charity to receive a bequest of $50,000. The balance of your estate ($500,000) is to go to your three children. Later on disaster strikes and your estate is essentially reduced to $100,000. Because of this specific bequest, if you die without changing your will, XYZ would still get $50,000 and your children would only receive about $17,000 each. Although there is nothing wrong with a specific bequest, it is important to change the specific details as your personal situation changes. You may also consider using percentage bequests instead.

Let's discuss probate. As mentioned previously, probate is the actual process in which a court oversees the distribution of property left by your will, and ensures that your directives are carried out. This is a very good thing, as it is the only way for the vast majority of people to ensure that the estate is distributed the way they want it to be done. If you want your cousin Billy Bob to receive your valuable beer can collection, the court will ensure that he gets the collection, or the will can not be closed. A typical situation usually involves heirs that include the surviving spouse and children. In this case, everything should run smoothly and relatively quickly. It generally takes only six to nine months to complete the process, although complicated or contested situations can last much longer. A valid and current will also expedites this process. Once again, if cousin Billy Bob has moved to the outback of Australia, the will can not be closed until the executor can prove to the court that Billy Bob received those beer cans!

Probate is not a four letter word, although many people feel that it is. At one time, almost all estates were required to undergo a formal probate. This procedure was often long and nightmarish. Fortunately, many states have since streamlined the process. There is often much less paperwork, time, and expense. Some states will even allow the estate representative to handle the process by mail. In approximately half the states, there is a flat fee for filing with probate court, ranging from $50 to $200. Other states set their fees based on the size of the probate estate.

It pays to research your state regulations and take some action. However, for most people the task of researching their states' regulations is basically unrealistic. When faced with the duties of an executor\executrix, they throw up their hands and run to the attorney that is in possession of the original will. They do not negotiate or shop for service and costs. Be proactive and ask questions. Shop around for a better deal. Because few states mandate a rigid fee schedule for probate, there is often a huge difference between what firms will charge, as well as the extent of services provided.

Step 4) Explore the world of trusts. Once all the basics have been attended to, if there are still some unanswered issues that need to be resolved, it may be appropriate to explore the use of trusts. Many people have huge misconceptions about trusts. They often believe that trusts are only for the wealthy because they are extremely expensive and the purchaser can never access the money if they need it. Some people also assume that you need to employ the services of a bank to start a trust fund. They immediately picture the marble floors and vaulted ceilings in which the assets will be locked away.

In reality, trusts do not have to cost that much. They can be extremely flexible and do not require the services of a bank. Many types of trusts are available, all designed to accomplish certain goals. Just as every individual will is crafted to fit the needs of a person, the same is true with trusts.

Without getting too technical, there are four types of trusts that will accommodate the majority of the population and their planning goals. The trusts include: testamentary, intervivos, revocable, and irrevocable. Testamentary and intervivos refer to when the trust is established. Testamentary means the trust is established upon the death of the person that has established the trust, also known as the grantor. Intervivos means the trust is established while the grantor is alive. Revocable means the grantor can usually change the trust at any time, to include the right to terminate the trust altogether. Irrevocable means that once activated, the trust can not be changed.

Testamentary trusts are used all the time by good planners. These types of trusts can be found within a will. Upon the death of the testator, the will directs a trust to be established, which will perform certain functions the testator has directed. These trusts often allow the testator to control assets and their distribution, possibly long after their death. A trust established for the benefit of minor children is a common example. The children may not be able to access the money until they reach a certain age or a particular event occurs in their life. For example, a child may receive the trust funds when he or she marries, begins a college education, or purchases a home. While you are alive, trusts do not cost any money. The trust does not really exist until the death of the grantor. At this time, the trust will be administered and costs may then be incurred.

Revocable trusts are often intervivos trusts. They are generally used to provide control for the grantor. They are excellent tools to help deal with any incapacity of an individual. The assets of these trusts are not subject to probate upon death. Lastly, although grossly oversold as a benefit, the terms of these trusts are private, which is unlike a will, because it is public information. (Of course, when was the last time you went to the courthouse to read about someone's will?) Many times these are sold as the infamous living trusts. Although a living trust can be a very good tool, they have often been oversold by hucksters looking to make money, not help people. As we said earlier, they can be wonderful tools, but make sure that you need one for the control purposes, and ensure that you are working with a good planner and attorney that will help you through the process of establishing and funding the trust.

Lastly, irrevocable trusts are commonly used to plan for reducing the impact of estate taxes. The key to understanding irrevocable trusts is that the trust has to be funded with some asset. That means you have to give assets away that you can never get back. If you do transfer assets to an irrevocable trust, then it is a true gift and you do not own it anymore. The government does not tax you on something that you do not own. These trusts are a way of giving things away (usually for tax reasons), but still maintaining control of the asset via the trust.

An Irrevocable Life Insurance Trust (ILIT) is a good planning tool that uses this concept. A life insurance policy on the life of the grantor is usually purchased by the trust. The policy could also be an existing policy which is gifted to the trust, although there are some ramifications to that approach. If the grantor owned the policy at death, the proceeds would be part of the taxable estate. With this technique, the policy is owned by the trust; therefore it is not an asset of the grantor. The grantor then makes an annual gift to the trust – normally equivalent to the annual premium for the policy. Upon death, the proceeds of the life insurance policy are not considered to be part of the grantor's estate, so the proceeds go to the beneficiaries, tax free. This is a wonderful tool if utilized in the right manner and situation.

Trusts can be great tools. They need not be expensive and can be individually tailored to your needs. Your authors, however, strongly recommend that you tend to Steps 1-3 before exploring the world of trusts. If you still feel you need to utilize other tools to accomplish your goals, it is imperative that you find a good planner and estate attorney that will make this happen.

As you approach retirement, make estate planning one of your goals. Whether or not you have a strong desire to leave assets to your heirs, most people don't have any desire to leave their assets to Uncle Sam. Perhaps you dread the thought of deciding who receives which assets. Regardless of your thoughts on estate planning, taking a passive approach and doing nothing is not wise. You may be unsure about some decisions at this time, but you probably do not want to leave your assets to the government. That is what may happen if you ignore estate planning. Think of it this way…do you really want to give more money to Uncle Sam?

Despite this fact, many people still tell us that they want to die as they are spending their last dollar. This may seem like an easy solution now, but we think you will sleep easier knowing that your affairs are in order and things will be taken care of when you are gone. You have worked hard all of your life. Do not let your precious assets get into the wrong hands. Thus, it is imperative that you take action now! Estate planning does not have to be a long, expensive, or an overwhelming task. View it as a process of going back to the basics and putting your assets to good use even after you are gone.

PUTTING TOGETHER THE RIGHT TEAM

Let's discuss the process of choosing which professionals to entrust your financial future. As with many aspects of life, trust is built over time. However, several key elements will help you find the type of professional that suits your personal situation.

Since this book is written by investment professionals, we will be exploring the process as it pertains to financial and investment planning. We will also be giving specific advice and direction on how to navigate that part of the process. Before we delve into the crux of the financial world, there are a few things that need to be said about attorneys, accountants, and financial advisors. One of the most troubling issues we encounter in our practice is when we hear a client say that they obtain their investment advice from their accountant or that they get their legal or tax advice from their broker or insurance agent. This is a recipe for disaster. Each of these professionals are trained, educated, and licensed in very different areas of the financial world, and the services that each can provide to their clientele are very different. Furthermore, the regulatory bodies that govern and monitor the conduct of these professionals are very different. The errors and omissions insurance (a sort of malpractice insurance) that each carries only covers them for their specific areas of professional expertise. In other words, if you are taking stock picks from your attorney or CPA, you may as well be getting them from your drycleaner or butcher because from a licensing standpoint, there is no difference.

The other important point to keep in mind about attorneys, accountants, and financial advisors is the significance of these professionals working together as a team. Each professional is licensed and educated to provide an important role in the financial planning process. The best way to ensure that your overall financial plan is being well addressed is to make certain that these professionals are communicating with each other about their individual contributions and working together in a cooperative manner. Because each of these professionals perceives financial planning from a different area of expertise, they often bring different perspectives to the process. This can be a very positive and productive aspect, as long as personal egos do not clash. Each professional should realize that he or she is a member of the team, with you as the star "quarterback."

Another thing to consider about the team approach is the importance of independence. Because tax, legal, and investment planning are so dependent upon one another, it is very common to see "one-stop-shops" that offer all three services. While this is not automatically bad, we do see this as problematic. We feel that the real strength of the team approach is when each professional brings his or her independent and unbiased expertise to your financial plan. Sometimes, if you have all three professionals working in the same facility and receiving compensation from the same source, it is difficult for these individuals to offer unbiased expertise. The concept of the team approach is not to have each member "singing from the same sheet music." Instead, the purpose is for these professionals to create a unique synergy that can only be achieved through team dynamics. We feel that independence is a very important part of this goal. Therefore, we recommend forming a team of separate professionals who can communicate and work together, while still maintaining their independence. Dedicating some extra time to finding the right professionals in the beginning will probably save you a lot of time, money, and frustration later.

The more complicated a person's financial situation is, the more likely they will need the services of a tax advisor, a legal advisor, and an investment advisor, all providing advice in their own areas of expertise. And let us be very clear about this… THEY ARE DIFFERENT AREAS OF EXPERTISE!

Assuming that we have succeeded in explaining how tax, legal, and investment professionals exist independently from one another, let's take a closer look into the world of financial advice. Although you will hear the term, "financial advisor" used rather frequently in the financial services industry, it is a very ambiguous term that applies to many different professionals who provide a variety of services. The title "financial advisor" does not really indicate what that person is qualified to do.

There are titles in the industry that are very specific to training and qualifications. Unfortunately, the financial industry has done a terrible job of educating the consumer about their particular meaning and differences. To complicate matters even further, there are more than 100 professional certifications and designations in the financial services world. These are the three or four letter abbreviations that you see beside the names of professionals. Some of these designations take a lot of time and dedication to achieve. On the other hand, some of them can be attained by attending a two or three hour class, or even by doing nothing except sending a few hundred dollars to a sham organization and buying the right to use the certification.

With all of the different titles, certifications, and designations being used today, how does the average consumer know who is best suited to help them with their unique needs and circumstances? Well, one way is by doing some research. We recommend visiting an excellent web site located at www.financial-designations.8m.com. You can research all of the existing professional licenses, certifications, and designations used in the industry. But…what if you do not want to spend hours and hours becoming an expert on financial credentials? Well, the good news is that there are two simple keys to understanding the financial services industry. If you understand these two points, you will be much better equipped to navigate your way through the sea of confusion and find the professionals who are best suited to help you. First, you should understand that there is a major difference between a **license** and a **certification**. Second, you should know the difference between **brokers** and **advisors**. We will address each of these differences.

Let's start with the difference between professional **licenses and certifications**. In simple terms, a professional license gives authority to conduct business in a certain field, while a professional certification (or designation) marks an academic achievement. Therefore, professional certifications do not give individuals the authority to conduct business at all.

At this time, we want to clarify an important point to avoid any misunderstandings or confusion. Our purpose is not to undervalue or minimize any professional certification or designation. We just want to bring some clarity to the very confusing world of financial advisors. As we mentioned earlier, some professional certifications and designations are very prestigious and require a significant amount of time, money, and dedication to attain. Some certifications, such as the ChFC, CFA, and MSFS are actually accredited degrees in the financial services field. When individuals have attained designations such as these, it shows they are serious about their chosen profession. Achieving this goal indicates that they want to be the best they can be in their career.

The problem is that for every designation which falls into that category, there are five or six more that can be attained by doing next to nothing. We see a real problem occurring when a slick salesperson purchases "tin star" designations, prints them on their business cards, and attempts to instantly gain the illusion of professionalism. We want to warn you about these types of individuals. The litmus test for whether someone is qualified to conduct business as a professional does not come from designations; it comes from a professional license.

To use a simple and corollary example, think about a medical doctor who is licensed to practice medicine as opposed to someone who has gone to the YMCA and became certified in First Aid or CPR. Is there a big difference? You bet there is. The same is true in the financial services industry; professional expertise is indicated by a professional license.

The reason we are taking so much time to illustrate this point is because of the huge amount of impropriety and dishonest sales practices that occurs in the financial services industry. There are people with all sorts of alphabet soup printed on their business cards offering financial advice they are not qualified to give. Before you let someone tell you to sell your stocks, move your retirement plan, or cash in your life insurance policies, you should be sure that person is LICENSED to give you that advice.

Why is licensing so important? There are several practical reasons:

- **Uniform requirements** – Everyone who holds a license in a particular field has completed the same criteria and testing to earn that license. You cannot purchase a license from a magazine advertisement or earn one from attending a one-hour seminar.

- **Continuing education** – Once an individual acquires a professional license, they are not set for life. As the industry changes, licensed individuals must maintain minimum continuing education requirements. Failure to do so could result in their license being revoked. This ensures that licensed individuals expand their knowledge as the financial world changes, and it also weeds out the "part timers".

- **Regulation and compliance** – In order to protect the consumer, a complex hierarchy of regulatory agencies and governing bodies monitor licensed professionals.

> These organizations supervise the conduct, sales practices, continuing education requirements and even the public advertising that are used by licensed individuals. Most importantly, if a licensed individual engages in unlawful activity, the regulatory agencies can fine, suspend, or even revoke that individual's license.

For all of these reasons, you probably understand why a professional license is important, especially when you are employing a particular individual to handle your finances. Do not hesitate to ask a professional about what licenses they hold and how long they have held them. Although licenses do not guarantee that an individual is ethical or competent, they do offer a level of protection in the event that you detect misconduct. We have provided more information and research sources in the appendix of this book to help you learn more about various licenses, designations, and regulatory agencies.

Let's now discuss the difference between brokers and advisors, another major aspect of understanding the financial services world. Financial professionals, regardless of their title, license, or designation, will fall into one of two major categories. They can provide brokerage services or they can provide advisory services. A professional can become licensed to provide both services, but there are distinct differences between the two, and separate licensing and registration are required for each. The practical differences are found in how the professional is compensated, and what services they are providing for that compensation.

Let's start by examining the brokerage business. Basically, the brokerage business is a commission business. A broker is a person or company that provides the sale of a product for a commission. In essence, there is nothing wrong with this. In fact, the brokerage business literally built the financial services industry. The insurance industry was developed by vast sales forces of insurance agents and brokers. The stock market was created by stock and investment brokers. We can imagine the same can be said of almost any industry. Once again, there is nothing bad about the brokerage business. However, you need to understand the fundamental purpose of the brokerage business is to sell products.

Our seminar attendees often share their personal stories of how they thought they were employing the services of a financial planner, but in actuality, this person just wanted to sell them insurance. A rather extreme example of this situation comes to mind. A couple approached us after a seminar to talk. They explained that they had worked with a team of "planners" that happened to work with a large and well-known insurance company. When the couple inquired about the cost of financial planning, the insurance agents explained to them that they do not charge for financial planning and only get compensated from any products that the client would buy. This sounded reasonable to the couple and they decided to proceed. Unfortunately, they followed the advice of these "planners" and implemented the "financial plan" that the two nice agents developed. We could clearly see the embarrassment and frustration on their faces when this couple explained that the "financial plan" was basically to purchase two very large whole life insurance policies and spend more than $40,000 per year to fund them. To make matters worse, these agents recommended that this couple stop funding their 401K plans and other retirement saving accounts so that they could afford these policies. Besides, according to these agents or "planners," the benefits of the insurance policies would be "much, much better."

In our opinion, this kind of conduct is criminal, and unfortunately, it is all too common. Worse yet, many of the companies who create and develop the financial products that are sold through the brokerage distribution systems advertise their products based on "high commission." This type of blatant emphasis on high commission means that the only products the consumer will ever see are the ones with the highest compensation to the broker. If a salesperson or broker receives a high commission from a product they market, you are paying for that in some respect. One of the dirtiest little secrets in the insurance and annuity business is that the longer an agent can get you to tie up your money with surrender charges and penalties, the more the agent will earn in commission. We have actually seen a case in which an agent sold a woman in her late 80s an annuity with a 15-year surrender charge period (meaning if she cancelled the policy at any time within 15 years, she would be charged a cancellation fee.). You could say that she was the ultimate optimist, but we think it is the result of an agent who desperately wanted to make a sale regardless if the product was an impractical choice for the client. We should also question the business practices of the annuity company for even issuing the contract!

Unethical brokers confuse and intimidate many consumers because consumers don't know who they can work with. The most damage occurs when an unsuspecting consumer falls for the agent's sales ploy and purchases expensive products they do not really need.

So then, what do you do when you want more than the sale of a product? Well that's where the advisory business, the other part of the financial services industry, enters into the picture. We defined the brokerage business as the sale of a product for a commission. The advisory business could be described as the sale of fee-based planning services. In the advisory business, a Registered Investment Advisor charges a fee for the development of a financial plan. Advisors could charge a flat fee, an hourly rate, or base their costs upon the amount of assets managed. An advisor should focus on solving problems, addressing needs, and developing solutions for your financial plan. The way that we like to describe the process is that you and the advisor get on the same side of the table, roll up your sleeves, and get to work creating a detailed plan of how you will make your financial dreams come true. If you decide to make changes or buy products, it should be because the plan has clearly identified reasons for doing so. With this approach, you never need to second guess your financial decisions or worry about whether or not you were sold the correct products. Any additional products you do purchase are the tools required to make your financial plan a blueprint for success.

As you can probably see, the brokerage and the advisory business seem to be very different from one another. In fact, the licensing required for each industry also varies, as well as the regulatory agencies that monitor the conduct of these professionals. A licensed broker is not necessarily licensed to provide fee-based planning and a planner may, but is not necessarily licensed to help you buy or sell securities or insurance products. However, many professionals hold both types of licensing and registration since most people need both types of services at some point in their financial lives.

We want to warn you about two things in the advisory side of the financial services industry. First, make sure the person who claims they are a licensed advisor actually is a licensed advisor. Having legal authority to provide fee-based planning requires much more than simply printing the word "advisor" on a business card.

If a professional wants to charge for investment related advice, he or she must first comply with the specific licensing, examination and registration requirements governing Registered Investment Advisors. These requirements are created and enforced by both state and federal securities laws. Qualified professionals who provide these services can be Registered Investment Advisors themselves, or Advisory Representatives of a corporate Registered Investment Advisor firm. Pay close attention to the wording when researching an individual's qualifications. This is very important considering how loosely the term "Financial Advisor" is used. Remember that "financial advisors" are not necessarily Registered

Investment Advisors. Registered Investment Advisors have greater fiduciary responsibilities than brokers, and also must comply with additional disclosure requirements. All Registered Investment Advisors must provide their clients with a special disclosure document called Form ADV. The ADV contains mandatory disclosures of licensing, registrations, fee schedules, disciplinary actions, and more. The quickest way to determine if someone holding themselves out as an Investment Advisor is genuine is by asking them for their Form ADV. You can research more about Investor Advisor rules and regulations by visiting your States Security Commission web site.

The second warning is to make sure you actually have the opportunity to work with the licensed professional who creates your plan. Oftentimes, some large organizations have representatives who sell planning services for the firm. This company then sends your financial information to a "planning mill" in another state and an unknown person you've never actually met creates your "financial plan." Approximately six weeks later, you receive a 3-inch thick leather binder that costs you $1,000. Then, the local broker tells you what to buy. This service is not exactly our idea of working with a licensed professional. Since everyone has different financial goals, find a firm that will work closely with you and make you part of the process. Communication and interaction are very important components of the financial planning process.

Remember that the best way to protect yourself is through education. If you are aware of how the financial industry operates, you will begin to discover which services will meet your needs. The brokerage business is perfect for the delivery of product, providing that you do your homework and deal with the right professional. When your needs dictate planning over product sale, the advisory business is there to help. Be sure to use a licensed, Registered Investment Advisor who will give you personalized attention and help you customize a plan that meets your unique needs. All in all, remember that using a professional means that you are seeking assistance, not relinquishing control. In our strong opinion, you should always remain captain of the ship, especially since these financial decisions involve your money and your future, and you are the one that will ultimately have to live with your choices.

Here are a few final thoughts on choosing a financial professional. First, personal referrals are worth their weight in gold. If you know anyone who is in a similar situation as yourself, ask them if they are satisfied with their financial professional. If you are preparing to retire from a company, contact associates who have also recently retired and find out if they could recommend a financial professional. This old proverb strongly applies in this scenario: "If you do right by someone, they will tell someone about it. If you do wrong by someone, they will tell a hundred people." Obtaining personal referrals as well as asking for references of existing clients is always a good start to your financial planning journey.

Secondly, shop around. Everyone is a unique individual with different personalities and characteristic traits. An advisor can be totally competent, but if the two of you are not able to communicate on a comfortable level, the relationship will probably not work. You do not need to be best friends with your advisor, but you do need to have a cordial working relationship. Occasionally, personalities just do not mix. If that happens, keep looking until you find someone who you can address your financial needs, concerns, and fears. This is what the financial planning process is all about.

Finally, when you do find the right financial advisor, recommend him or her to your friends and family. Promoting the "good guys" through word of mouth is the best way to help the professionals who are out there doing a good job, while also helping others who need competent, ethical advice.

Pulling It All Together

Throughout the course of this book, we have discussed a tremendously diverse and complicated array of subject matter. We did this in a way that was meant to weed out the minutia and speak directly about the fundamentals. We share the belief of Vince Lombardi, the great Hall of Fame football coach, who taught that mastery of the fundamentals accounted for 90 percent of success. "Focus on the fundamentals…and you're assured of success."

However, there is still one more component of building an effective and dependable financial plan. This final step is the one that proves to be most challenging and perhaps, the most important. **We want you to take the knowledge that you have learned and apply it to the planning for your financial future**. In our years of practicing financial planning, it has become clear that this skill separates bad planners from good planners and, hence, will end up defining the success, or lack of success, of one's investment efforts. Having all the facts in the world will not help you unless you can apply that information in a way that addresses all of your needs, and coordinates action in a productive and complimentary way.

This is very similar to the lesson that we learned from Dale Carnegie -- it was the ability to coordinate and manage the skills of others that he used to build an empire. Similarly, it is the ability to integrate each of the subjects that we have just discussed into a synergistic and well-oiled plan that will allow us to build a successful retirement.

So, how do you accomplish this? How do you bring it all together?

In order to tackle this final question, let us revisit the last paragraph of our introduction to this book: "It will become evident throughout the course of your study that properly addressing all the areas of financial concern in a functional and effective way does involve a great amount of care and skill. If it starts to seem overwhelming…take heart. Knowing your desired outcome is half the battle. The information provided in each of the preceding chapters has shown you how to get on and stay on the right track. Now that you have a good grasp of the fundamentals, you can clearly define the goals and aspirations of your own financial plan and know how to get the help you need in each area."

To do this, you actually need to begin with the end results you want. Any good plan in life should be oriented towards the end goal. You have an advantage because you chose the first step by educating yourself in the key area of retirement planning. You should now have a fairly good understanding of the fundamental components of retirement planning.

- Choosing the Right Pension Option
- Social Security/Medicare/Medicaid
- Retirement and Income Taxes
- Maintaining Lifestyle and Not Outliving Your Income
- Managing Risk
- Protecting Your Family

- Preventing Medical and Long Term Care Costs from Consuming Your Retirement Assets
- Basic Estate Planning

In other words, you know that retirement planning is more than picking a pension payout, applying for your Social Security, and buying a fishing pole. With the understanding of the fundamentals, you can now intelligently and realistically define specific retirement goals. As you consider the type of lifestyle that you want to maintain, you and your spouse should ponder a variety of questions. Here are some examples:

- Do you want to travel?
- Will you downsize to a smaller home?
- Will you continue to work? If so, will you work full-time or part-time?
- Do you plan on relocating?
- How important is it to leave an inheritance to your children or heirs?
- How would the need to receive special medical care or assistance affect your plans?

You must spend time reflecting on and discussing each of these issues. Once you get a realistic vision of how you want to live your retirement, you can determine the amount of income you will need to sustain your desired lifestyle. If you find that your current plan does not support your goals, you may need to adjust your spending, investment strategy, or taxes. Once these have been examined, you can define action steps and make decisions. You can also examine what can go wrong with your plan, and prepare for protection components.

Throughout this book, we also stressed the importance of obtaining help from a professional when necessary. We advocate the approach of Carnegie. He chose to be a "manager" instead of an "expert." If you still disagree with this solution and wish to completely devise a retirement plan on your own, please realize that you will need to read an entire library of books on financial planning. Each of the eight tentacles of retirement planning that we have discussed has an enormous breadth of information associated with it. As mentioned previously, the intent of this book is to cover the fundamentals and point you in the right direction, not to make you an expert on any of the topics we discussed. Furthermore, you must remember that each of the subjects is dynamic in nature. Products, laws, tax codes, and regulations continue to change. For this reason, being an "expert" is not a destination; it is an ongoing process. We do not recommend tackling the topic of retirement planning alone.

As you probably guessed, we are not fans of the lone wolf mentality. Let us also say that we practice what we preach. Although we may consider ourselves to be experts in retirement planning, we do not pretend to be experts on tax law, estate law, offshore accounts, real estate speculation, or commodities trading, even though those fall under the umbrella of "financial planning." In other words, we stay dedicated to our area of expertise and consult other professionals when necessary.

Since we strongly believe in hiring a group of professionals to assist you, we will spend the remainder of this chapter discussing how to create and manage a team of financial professionals. These experts will help you develop and maintain your retirement strategies. Unfortunately, there is no "connect the dots" or step by step way to achieve this goal. Instead, we will share with you a list of priorities.

Who should be on your team? - While the exact makeup of your financial team will depend on your individual circumstances, the three primary professionals that most people need to consult include tax, legal, and investment advisors. How much time and work you need from each will once again depend upon your situation. You may only need to work with an attorney to create a will and estate plan. If your tax advisor helps with taxes, then you would probably meet with that professional at least once a year. However, if you do your own taxes, you may require less frequent contact with this professional. Business and investment property owners, on the other hand, probably need regular contact with their tax advisor.

Because our occupation involves investment advice and financial planning, we are generally the "key advisor" to our clientele. Normally, we meet with our clients at least each quarter to monitor their investment portfolios and update their retirement plans. For this reason, we are usually the team component with whom you will have the most contact. We often coordinate the other members of the team in terms of meetings, tasks, and progress reports. In addition to these three professionals, many people like to have a mortgage broker, property and casualty insurance specialist, or a long-term care expert as part of their team. Once again, look closely at your own circumstances and build an appropriate team. If you do not know who to consult in a particular area, ask a team member that you already know and trust to recommend other professionals.

Team attitude - Personal egos of team members should not interfere with your needs. Your professional advisors are supposed to help you, not compete among one another.

Because estate, tax, and investment planning operate so closely together and may, at times, overlap, it will be common for each team member to have an opinion at times that may contradict another professional. There is nothing wrong with this. In fact, because each professional has different training, licensing, and education, each will view an issue from a different perspective. You can actually benefit from these diverse viewpoints! By considering the opinion of each advisor, you can make a more informed decision. However, each professional must behave in a consultative manner and not turn your financial future into a competition.

Also, remember that licensing makes a difference. As investment advisors, we may have our own opinions on a tax or estate plan, but we are not going to pretend we know more than a CPA or an attorney. We know we can provide expert advice in our fields. Therefore, we must respect the fact that other professionals may also present information from a different perspective. This type of healthy respect among team members is essential to a successful retirement planning team.

Team approach vs. one-stop shopping – In order to elaborate on the previous point, we also want to emphasize the importance of independence. We have been discussing the need to build a team that can work together in order to help you address, coordinate, and take action on each aspect of your retirement plan. We have also stated that each professional offers unique education and training, which can benefit you if managed properly.

As you search for the right professionals, you may encounter firms that house an accountant, attorney, and investment planner all under the same business entity. While this may seem appealing for the purpose of convenience and communication, it can cause some problems, as very often these professionals work together because they share common views on matters. In other words, independent and impartial professional opinions may be compromised, even inadvertently, when team members earn fees and commissions from the same source. We believe that objective professional talents are essential to the team approach. We suggest that you find independent professionals who can work together while maintaining their own independence and professional integrity.

Clear and frequent communication – When all critical areas of a financial plan are addressed, and you have the help you need to stay on track, little should go wrong. We have found that the problems that do occur are usually a result of poor communication. Financial planning is an on-going process, and as the captain of your team, you need to be kept abreast of issues as they progress. We previously mentioned that we meet with our retirement clients at least once a quarter. At those meetings, we assess every single aspect of their investments. In addition, we do a thorough review of their overall tax, estate, insurance, and will planning at least once a year. This may seem like overkill at first, but we always have plenty to discuss at our meetings. The fact is…things change…especially investments, tax laws, and family circumstances. Sometimes, these changes are negative, such as declining health, market losses, financial emergencies, or other challenges. In other instances, financial aspects need adjusted because of positive changes like investment growth or additions to the family. The point is that life can change at any moment. Your financial team is in a unique position to view these aspects from a different perspective. This group of professionals should ensure that you are attending to the right things at the right times. Clear and frequent communication is the key to this process.

Plan before products –All too often, people focus so much on the minute details of products that they lose sight of the bigger picture. They focus heavily on expenses or ratings, but forget about lifestyle needs, inflation, and protection. This can also occur with other situational decisions like creating a will or minimizing taxes. An individual's decisions can become so isolated and myopic because they do not consider all of the important factors.

The most significant aspect of our firm's philosophy that we hold sovereign is the need to start with a thorough and comprehensive plan before making decisions. Many times, prospective clients will approach our firm with a sum of money to invest or a product they want to acquire, but they have not defined long-term goals or needs. We do not work with individuals that put the cart before the horse. We do not know what your needs are unless we step back and put the plan in proper perspective. As we have stated before, this is the single most important aspect of building a successful retirement.

Dynamics and flexibility – Another key characteristic of a great retirement plan is built-in flexibility. Life changes fast, and your retirement plan needs to be able to adapt. We talked about subjects such as surrender charges, fees, penalties, managing risk, taxes, and protection. These aspects must have the ability to be easily changed within your plan. If you have an emergency situation, you do not want to pay enormous fees or suffer tax consequences just to access your money. You also do not want to find yourself being forced to cash in investments when they are down in value because you never planned for unexpected events. Nor do you want to wait until you are in poor health before planning for long-term care or medical expenses. These are just a few examples of how an inflexible plan or poor timing can create disaster. Because of this, you must pay special attention to the dynamics of the products, accounts, and contracts that you choose. When making any financial decision, considering "how easy is it to change" should be forefront in your mind.

Let's take one more look at the philosophy of Carnegie. This historical figure did not build a fortune and master the steel industry by becoming an expert at each and every aspect of manufacturing, selling, and distributing steel. He shaped his empire by managing men who knew how to perform these tasks. He was a manager, not an expert. We suggest that you take the same attitude when planning your retirement journey.

In closing, remember that there are some things in life that you cannot control. You can only influence certain issues. That is really the message of this book. Focus on the correct areas; keep the fundamentals in perspective; and stay informed as much as possible. Financial planning is not rocket science; it just involves task management and proper planning. We sincerely wish that this book has helped you discover a more clear vision of what you can do to meet your retirement goals. Use this book as a guide and transform your ambitions into reality.

Many others may have to simply rely on good luck as they attempt to meet their retirement goals. Applying the information in this book to your personal situation takes you beyond this point. Knowledge is power. Because you are now armed with some knowledge, you have a better chance to meet your goals. Also, as with any good news, spread the word! Let others know the insights you have learned. They will thank you, and so will we.